How to Rent
Vacation
Properties
By Owner

How to Rent
Vacation Properties
By Owner

The Complete Guide to Buy, Manage,
Furnish, Rent, Maintain and Advertise your
VACATION RENTAL INVESTMENT

Christine Hrib Karpinski

Cover design by George Foster
Interior design by Desktop Miracles, Inc.

Publisher's Cataloging-in-Publication Data

(Prepared by The Donohue Group, Inc.)

Karpinski, Christine Hrib.
    How to rent vacation properties by owner / Christine Hrib Karpinski.

      p. : forms ; cm.
    Includes bibliographical references and index.
    ISBN: 0–9748249–0–9

    1. Vacation rentals--Handbooks, manuals, etc. 2. Vacation homes. 3. Real estate development. I. Title. II. Title: Vacation properties.
HD7289.2 K37 2004
643.2

Printed in the United States of America

to Tom with all my love . . .

Table of Contents

Foreword

Home Sweet Vacation Home:
The Mother Lode of Real Estate Investments

By Broderick Perkins, DeadlineNews.Com

The so-called "New Economy"—the 1990s' technology-driven, record-setting, longest economic expansion ever—ended abruptly with the dawn of the New Millennium.

The Recession of 2001 that followed lasted less than a year, but in the wake of the downturn dot combustion scorched retirement savings, torched personal fortunes and turned small investments into large piles of ashes.

Meanwhile, the housing market emerged unscathed, thanks to more than a decade of home-equity growth through the economic expansion. It was as if the recession never existed.

Housing has not only maintained it's position as the centerpiece of the American Dream, it revealed its status as a cornerstone of the national economy—when the economy needed it most.

Consumer spending is what drives the economy and a growing share of consumer spending today is generated by growing home equity wealth.

During the economic growth period of the 1990s, home price appreciation increased nationwide by an average of approximately 43 percent, according to the Office of Federal Housing Enterprise Oversight. In just the past five years, the average rate of home price appreciation has nearly matched that of the 10 previous years, rising another 41 percent.

What sounds like an astounding rate of relentless appreciation is small potatoes compared to the growth in vacation home values.

In a first of it's kind survey of home values in select housing markets researchers found that values have increased at about twice the rate of new and existing homes nationwide.

In 2004, when EscapeHomes.com examined real estate agent and MLS data from 10 popular vacation home markets, it found that median home prices rose from $419,000 in 2003 to $511,000 during the second quarter this year—a 22 percent increase.

During the same period the National Association of Home Builders saw the median price of existing homes nationwide rise from $187,900 to $209,900, a nearly 12 percent increase, while the National Association of Realtors (NAR) reported an increase in the median home price of new homes from $175,000 to $191,800, a 9 percent increase.

Given the potential for such a return, it's not surprising that a growing share of vacation homes are purchased as investment properties—20 percent of all second home properties purchased in 1999, compared to 37 percent in 2002, were purchased as investment properties, according to NAR.

Vacation homes could very well be the mother-of-all investments for numerous reasons.

Perhaps the first big boon to the vacation home market came with the 1997 Taxpayer Relief Act. It's liberal relaxation of capital gains tax rules began to allow home sellers to keep and spend a large share of their profits as they wished, without requiring them to roll it over into another home. Many cashed out of larger homes and used the proceeds to invest in a smaller home—or two—often a vacation home for active retirement.

Baby Boomers, who'd been homeowners for decades and had accumulated equity wealth, were most likely to benefit from such tax relief and they get credit for really pumping up vacation home demand.

Boomers, Americans born between 1946 and 1964, represent a population bulge of 75 million people who are redefining the second half of life as an active period of semi- or non-retirement, rather than a sedentary one. The hard-working, self-made, Peter Pan generation of Baby Boomers enjoy career-made incomes, successful investments, home equity gains and empty-nests. More and more often they want smaller homes in vibrant communities—so much so that they have already turned some vacation home markets into high-end resorts.

That's reflected in a growing number of surveys of "top" vacation home markets that are not the same old resorts, but more and more often lists of "emerging" vacation home markets that give buyers "insider" investment information.

Also, the growing vacation property market was one of few sectors in the travel industry to get an unintended boost from 911 after a fearful nation of travelers decided to stick closer to home and take more domestic vacations. Those travelers discovered both a greater feeling of security and a better more homey travel value in vacation homes—compared to traditional hotel and motel resort accommodations.

Finally, as more travelers sought out vacation home lodging, hard-socked stock market investors also were encouraged to move into real estate and cash in on the demand.

Existing and emerging supply-and-demand economics likely will continue to drive the lucrative vacation home market and along with it, the returns on vacation home investments.

However, if you want to compound your return, you can't rest on the market's laurels.

Along with information about the basic economic forces that drive the vacation home market, you also need to develop a strategy to actively manage your investment.

To produce the best financial return, it takes time, insight, attention to detail and a lot of do-it-yourself drive.

Take the time.

You already hold the rest of the strategy in your hands.

It's called *How To Rent Vacation Properties By Owner* by Christine Hrib Karpinski.

Just don't forget to kick back once in a while, vacation in your vacation home and reap all the benefits.

Broderick Perkins, is executive editor of San Jose, CA-based DeadlineNews.Com, an editorial content and consulting firm. Perkins has been a consumer and real estate journalist for 25 years.

Preface

I could not afford to buy a vacation property, but . . . I wanted one anyway. During my quest, I stumbled upon a vital loophole that rarely surfaces when looking to purchase vacation property—"Renting by Owner." Unfortunately, there aren't many resources out there to provide much-needed answers on how to take advantage of this oft-overlooked, and as I found out, important loophole. So, I wrote this book to fill the void.

I bought the vacation home of my dreams, and I spent more for it than I did for my primary residence. I have never regretted it. I had positive cash flow from day one. Others became curious and asked if I would share my knowledge. I did. Word of mouth spread, and I started giving seminars to teach people how to own a vacation property and rent it themselves.

These pages are filled not only with my own observations and experiences, but also with true stories I've compiled from conversations with hundreds of owners. Over the years, they have opened up and shared with me their challenges and triumphs. I've changed their names for privacy reasons, but you will find a treasure trove of wisdom in their anecdotes. Whatever situation you become involved with, fear not . . . you're not alone. The people I've worked with have found innovative strategies that really work. Now you can benefit from their experiences as well.

I hope you enjoy reading this book as much as I enjoyed writing it. Owning a vacation home and managing it yourself is an exciting adventure. And I want to be there to help you every step of the way.

Acknowledgements

Wow ... finally complete. This book took much more work than I ever anticipated. It has been a long, arduous and fun journey. I can't take all the credit there are many people for whom without their help and support, this book would not have ever been accomplished.

For The Personal Help and Encouragement

First and foremost to my loving husband and best friend, Tom. Thanks for the constant encouragement and loving support. Thanks for believing in me. And thanks for the constant supply of Bon-Bons. Tom, I love you.

To my son Zachary, who dealt with mom sitting at the computer and talking on the phone many, many hours everyday. Thanks for understanding mom's work and your help with cooking dinners and household chores. Zach I love you!

To my father Mihaly Hrib, who through your own actions taught me how much hard work and perseverance can achieve. I'm sure that you are walking around heaven saying, "See I did not have the opportunity to go to school, I never learned to read, but my daughter (fer), I made sure she had a good education." Dad, I wish you could have lived to see this book come to fruition. I know you are proud.

To my Mom, Judy Hrib Kowalewski, you made me who I am today. No words can explain the impact you have on me. You are my hero. I miss you everyday. I am sure you are looking down, smiling at the irony of your little girl that was always in trouble at school for talking too much. Look Mom, I speaking for a living now!

To my in-laws, Ed and Shirley Karpinski, thanks for your encouragement and assistance. You are wonderful parents to both Tom and me.

To Pappa John Kowalewski, for your inspirational words. You encouraged me to take the risk to do what I love. You always remind me, if the love for your work runs out, then move onto the next thing, but not until the love runs out.

To my very special Aunt, Diana Paradise, Thanks for your spiritual guidance. For your willingness to help in all possible ways, and for your constant words of encouragement through out my life. You have truly inspired me.

To all my good friends, especially, Dianne, Dede, Gabbi, Gai Lynn, Karen, Karlene, Kim, Maria and Tania.

For The Professional Help and Encouragement

To my friend Dianne Dhanani, who helped us buy and rent our first vacation property. With out your honest candidness, we would have never purchased. And there would be no story to write.

Thanks to all the vacation property owners that attended my seminars and encouraged me to write this book. Thanks too to those that took the time to answer my survey and and shared your stories, experiences, ideas and tips.

And to the vacation property web site owners, thanks for your input and assistance. Your dedication to the industry has made it possible for each individual owner to successfully rent their vacation homes.

A special thanks to all the information contributors, especially Jack Simpson, thanks for the many articles you allowed me to quote. You were the pioneer of "by Owner" in the Destin area. To Amy

Greener, thanks for your experiences and talents and sharing them in this book. To Jeff Cutler, Jeff Desich, George Jaremko, and Gai Lynn McCarthy, thanks for your articles and input.

Gratitude to all my great friends and collogues who, for the meager salary of one red pen, agreed to proof read this book. Dave Clouse, Edward Karpinski, Kim Land, Hunter Mellville, Karen Pollack, Sheryl Pollack, Fred Quinn, and Jennifer Shriver.

Thanks to all who helped me put my book together. Stephen O'Brien for help with my initial outline. Cover designer George Foster of Foster and Foster. Layout designer Barry Kerrigan of Desktop Miracles. Final Editor Celia Rocks of Rocks-DeHart Public Relations. Transcriber Maria Pembrook.

A special thanks to all those who helped the first print run of this book sell out in 5 months! Celia Rocks and Dottie DeHart of Rocks-De Hart Publications.

Thanks to all the Vacation Rental By Owner portal sites who helped spread the word about this book. The links are appreciated. A special thanks goes to Hunter Melville of cyberrentals.com.

Thanks to Bart Meltzer of rent1online.com for contributing new articles for the second printing.

And finally a special Thank You to Broderick Perkins for the wonderful foreword.

Most importantly, I thank the Lord for the gifts and blessings bestowed upon me.

1

Getting Started

It always sounded like a great idea, didn't it? Owning a vacation home. You heard your friends talking about the possibilities. "It pays for itself," they said, and that part of it really appealed to you. After all, it only makes sense. Why spend thousands of dollars on hotels when you can own the vacation home of your dreams, spend as many weeks as you want every year enjoying it, then rent it out the rest of the year, and rake in all that income. Well, I'm here to tell you that you've made an excellent decision. But (you knew there would be a "but") don't delude yourself into thinking this will be simple, easy, or without risks. You need someone to guide you through the process, to show you the ins and outs of how it all works, the pitfalls to avoid, and how to earn maximum profits. If you do things the right way—by educating yourself before jumping in blindly—you will be much better off in the long run.

The first question you need to answer is this: are you buying a vacation property for your own personal use or for an investment? Before you answer, I want to let you in on a little secret: you can do both! In fact, people who otherwise would not be able to buy a vacation home can indeed if they learn the right techniques of renting by owner. This is not for the wealthy only, and it's certainly not a get-rich-quick scheme. It's a time proven strategy that almost any middle-income family can use effectively. I will show you how your property can pay for itself (see "break-even formula" in Chapter 3). It's not as difficult as you might think. My goal is to teach you how to own a vacation home that will be a financial asset rather than a liability.

Think of this new venture you're embarking on as a unique hybrid. You're marrying the idea of owning a vacation home for yourself with the idea of renting it out to others and keeping it as a long-term investment. So, when you do decide to move forward, the decisions you make will be both financial *and* emotional. Remember back when you bought the home you live in now? Was it just a financial decision? Of course not. You knew that everything had to be right, had to have a certain feel to it before you took the big plunge and made an offer. The location was a key, for sure, but there were other factors: the number of bedrooms, the size and condition of the lot, the garage, the basement, fireplaces, the kitchen cabinets, the wallpaper, paint . . . the list is almost endless. But all of these things mattered tremendously to you, because, after all, this was going to be where you lived, the place you came home to after a long day's work to unburden yourself and relax, the place where you entertained friends, and, quite possibly, the place where you raised your children and gathered your family for holidays for many years. So a lot more went into your decision than just the asking price.

It's much the same when it comes to buying vacation property. A lot of thinking has to go into it. And while it's true that you spend a certain amount of time planning your vacation trips (deciding on the best airfares, hotels, rental cars, etc.) don't think of buying a vacation home as simply a minor extension of that process. It is, in fact, an entirely different process. It's not just a one-shot vacation where you go for a week, hopefully have a good time, and then head home. Not at all. Buying a vacation home, whether for an investment or for personal use, usually means a long-term commitment. And, if it is for personal use, the stakes are a lot higher. It becomes more than a simple matter of what kind of return you get on your investment. Whatever you do, don't think of this as similar to dabbling in stocks or any other kind of investing. Instead, think of it in the same terms as when you were buying your primary residence. I know you won't be living there year round, but in all likelihood, you will still be making a large emotional investment in this property. It is not just some impersonal hotel where you hang out for a little while, and then you're gone. This is the place you'll be going for that much needed rest and relaxation over and over again every year, probably several times each year. Its location, size, and condition are important, serious issues. These decisions cannot be made lightly.

Try to cover all of your bases. What about personal emergencies? What if there is a major problem with your primary home (the septic system goes, you are flooded, etc.)? What if you or your spouse loses a job? It's not an unrealistic possibility in today's hard-to-predict economic environment. For the most part, there is no such thing as a stable job these days.

I'm not asking these questions to scare you. I just want you to go into this new venture with your eyes wide open. But there's no reason to worry that this is somehow the equivalent of going to Vegas and betting your life's savings at the craps table. Far from it. Here's what real estate expert Jack Simpson said on the subject, "Trying to eliminate risks often creates other risks. Some people put all their money in a 'safe' insured account only to see their buying power taken away by taxes and inflation. Ask yourself, what is the worst that can happen?

To me, the worst thing is seeing your life slip by without risk and reward. That's sad."

Are there challenges to owning a vacation home? Yes, and they will vary greatly from one person to another. Be sure to bring your family situation into the picture. Do you have children? Do you or your spouse have demanding jobs? People are so busy these days, many of us don't even have enough time to mow one lawn, never mind two! Even if you hire landscapers and other helpers (and the money can add up fast) to assist with maintaining the property, when it comes right down to it, you, as the owner, will still have to spend at least a few weekends a year at the place making sure everything is in proper order. Do you have that kind of time? Even if you do, is that something you're *willing* to do? Maybe you're just too darned tired to spend your time that way. Be honest with yourself about these things before making any decisions. I'm sure you've heard the term "sweat equity." Well, it really plays an important role when it comes to owning a vacation home and renting it yourself. This is something you have to rely on yourself to do. Nobody else can do it for you. Size up the situation carefully before taking the next step. The challenges are not by any means overwhelming . . . *if* you have the right information for dealing with them, which is why, in the following chapters, I will arm you with all of the facts you will ever need to know about vacation home ownership and renting by owner.

Well, I see you're still reading so you must have decided to keep going. Good. Remember, this is supposed to be fun, even though it involves hard work. But if you've gone this far, you're ready to answer another very important question: where will this vacation home be? The old real estate cliché—"location, location, location"—is extremely pertinent at this point. Don't jump to an overly simplistic conclusion such as, "Well, I live in Michigan, and I hate these horrible, snowy, freezing winters we have every year. I'll buy a vacation home in sunny south Florida where I can escape with the kids every February vacation. Man, that'll be the life!"

Well . . . maybe. Then again, maybe not. Have you really thought that plan through? You're talking about a trip of over 1,000 miles. You can't get there easily by car. Every time you need to visit your property, for any reason, chances are you'll have to fly. And while there may be lots of cut-rate airfares these days, it's still not cheap, and it's certainly not convenient. Getting a direct flight can be nearly impossible. Tedious layovers and connections, not to mention all of the post-9/11 security hassles and long lines, can leave you exhausted well before you even arrive at your home away from home's doorstep. Is that what you want? I'm not exaggerating. Having a vacation home in some exotic locale far from home may have a strong appeal, but it's not too practical. I recommend limiting your prospects to places within a six-hour drive of where you live.

You also need to do a good deal of research about the location before making a selection. It's not like you can throw a dart at the map and just take your chances. Even if you're buying the vacation home primarily for personal use, you have to know and understand the market. Just because it is located on a beautiful lake or has a breath-taking view of the ocean, doesn't necessarily mean it is a good deal. What is the rental history of the house? What is the competition like? Is the area glutted with vacation homes? How long is the busy season? These and many other questions are crucial to ask—and answer—before you make any decisions. Do your homework!

Again, personal choices will play a large role. Think about the vacations you have taken for the last 10 years. Actually, write them down; it will make it easier to keep track of things. Where did you go? The mountains? The oceans? The woods? Did you go to quiet places? Somewhere you could lie in a hammock all day and read a book? Or, exciting places with lots of nightlife and fun attractions to visit? Now imagine you had to choose just one of those locations, and that is where you will, from now on, be spending your vacations. Does anywhere in particular come to mind? Hopefully, this winnowing process will give you some clues as to the kind of places you should be searching for.

OK, so we've gone through the preliminaries: your motivations for buying, and whether your circumstances make this a sensible move for you. Let's assume you've determined that vacation home ownership is indeed the right way to go. Now you have to get ready for the long haul, which means you need to come to the realization that this is a long-term commitment. This isn't the kind of deal where you are going to do a quick flip, i.e., invest a little money, make a few improvements, and cash out way ahead of the game. I'm not saying that it can't be done, and in some cases I've seen people do it quite successfully. But for the average vacation homebuyer, that is not going to be the route you take.

Instead, you should look it at this way: the investment that you'll be making will enable you to afford a property that you couldn't otherwise afford. The one constant in real estate is that it almost always appreciates, and sometimes it does so very quickly. If you play it smart, you may build up a good deal of equity in just a few short years. Yes, at first you might have to rent it out for most of the year just to break even. It probably won't be a cash cow, so don't set your expectations too high. However, with a little patience, as the years go by and the equity continues to build and rents increase, you will be able to rent the property less often and still stay ahead of the game. It will eventually become profitable, and in the meantime, you have a wonderful place where you can spend your future vacations. No reservation required.

Before we go too far, let me add a word of caution. They say politics is the art of compromise. Well, the same could be said of the real estate game, especially when it comes to vacation home ownership. We discussed earlier how this is not only a financial investment, but also an emotional investment. In other words, you have to really like the place before you go ahead and sign on the dotted line. And while that is certainly true, liking the place isn't the same as *loving* it. Yes, you want to be satisfied with it. You want it to be a place you are proud of and eager to visit. But you have to be realistic and acknowledge that sometimes you can't have everything that you want. For example, let's say you have a large family, and you really have your heart set on a five-bedroom house. However, through your extensive research of rentals in the area (see, you're taking my advice already), you've discovered that three bedrooms rent much better. Time for a compromise. Buy the three-bedroom (some of the kids will have to share, but they'll survive just fine), and put yourself in the best possible position for renting. Go with the situation that will really keep the cash flow up. The same thing happens when it comes to issues such as buying a furnished or unfurnished place. The latter means more work, of course, but in the end, it could be worth it. Explore all your options, and you will be glad you put in the extra effort. Compromises such as these will be neces-sary every step of the way—beach vs. just off the beach, condo vs. house, and many others. Just be prepared for these compromises, and you will be more likely to make intelligent, well-informed choices.

The bottom line to all of this, and a good credo to keep in mind as you begin this new adventure, is . . . you must be an actively involved owner! Get all the facts. You have to know what exactly it is you're buying, what the competition is, and who your potential renters are. This background work is well worth the effort because you'll soon be enjoying a vacation home that pays for itself. You may very well turn a profit. But, you must do your homework first. So keep reading.

Note: When people start considering the idea of buying vacation property, some people immediately think "timeshares." Let me say that that assumption is false. That is not what this book is about and, in fact, I see many disadvantages to timeshares and very few benefits. Think about it. When you buy a vacation property, you own it 52 weeks of the year. With a timeshare you only "own" it one week of the year. To me, that doesn't seem like true ownership. Moreover, they have no resale value at all. Let's say you buy a timeshare for $50,000. If you bought if for the whole year, what would the cost be? Do the math: 52 weeks x $50,000 = $2.6 million. Now take a close look at the property. Do you really think it is worth $2.6 million? I'm willing to bet it's not. You could probably buy a similar unit down the street for $200,000. So why would anybody get involved with this whole concept in the first place? It's usually the result of high-pressure sales tactics, which should be a sure sign right from the beginning that it's a bad idea for the buyer.

2

Financing Your Vacation Home

Everybody knows how to buy things. Most of us know how to find a bargain. When it comes to financing a home, suddenly all of our consumer savvy seems to disappear. Just mention the word *mortgage* and a great doubt descends on us like a huge dark cloud. Mortgages are the mysterious domain of bankers and other financial people—all that stuff about interest rates, fixed and flexible rates, closing costs, loan-to-debt ratios, fees and points, and the whole foreign language that goes with it. But there is indeed a way to cut through all of the confusion.

Let's look at it as if you were going to purchase a car. We've all done that before. Gives you a chill, doesn't it? The way those car salespeople double-talk you. Do you understand how they come up with the amount that they pay for your trade-in? Of course you don't. The whole sales pitch is designed to give you the impression that not only are you getting retail for your trade-in, but you're getting a great retail price on your new car. Wrong. At best, you're getting wholesale. But beyond that, there is the matter of buying the right car. There are choices to consider—make, model, color, seating capacity, accessories, etc. There are just as many different mortgage products out there as there are cars. Finding the right one, the one that best fits your needs, depends on the amount of research you are willing to do. But first, let me give you some psychology about getting a loan.

The first thing to realize is that your loan officer, counselor, broker, etc., whatever he or she calls him or herself, is a *salesperson*. The salesperson's main goal is to earn him or herself and the organization the biggest commission possible. I'm not telling you this so you will hate the salesperson, although it may be a reasonable assumption. Just as you educate yourself about cars prior to going to the dealership, you should do the same with your mortgage. Know all your options. By presenting yourself as an educated consumer, you will lessen your chances of being ripped off. The smarter you are, and the smarter you appear to be, the less likely you are to be taken for a ride.

The next thing is that most people never think in terms of *buying* a mortgage. It's always, "getting a loan" or "getting financed." Have you ever heard anyone say, "I'm *buying* a mortgage?" In this mindset of *getting* a loan, you, as the customer, are vulnerable and at a disadvantage. You probably feel that you have to convince the loan officer that you are worthy of a loan, as if he or she is doing you a favor. It is very important to have the correct mindset! Remember the loan officer needs your business as much as you need the loan.

The first thing that people always shop for is rates. Mortgage rates are determined through some very in-depth formulas based on all sorts of numbers that we as consumers really do not need to understand. Bottom line, you just want to know what's the best rate available *for you*. Mortgage rates are quoted in increments of eighths or 0.125 increments, for example: 6.00, 6.125, 6.25, and 6.375, or 6, 6⅛, 6¼, and 6⅜.

Now let's say you shop around, check the rates on a particular day, and find that various mortgage companies have all different rates for the same type of loan. Why is this? Well, if you view mortgages just like any other consumer product, say cars, then depending on where dealers purchase the car (from the manufacturer, used car auctions, wholesale, etc.) dealers can price the cars according to the discounts they may receive when they purchase the vehicles. This gives car dealers the leverage to charge more or less for the same exact vehicle as their competitors. The same is true for mortgages. Certain mortgage companies do more volume in one product so their lender (supplier) sells that product at a discount rate, thus making it easier for the mortgage company to sell it to the consumer for less.

But I caution you, rate *is not* the only thing to consider when shopping "to purchase" a loan. You need to consider rates, products, *and* fees, the same as you would consider different makes, models, and accessory packages for a car. Don't make the mistake of thinking that there is anything standard about fees. No, absolutely not! There are many fees that are fixed, such as doc stamps on a deed, taxes, and title insurance. However, there are many fees that are not fixed and will vary from lender to lender, such as loan origination fees, discount fees, appraisals, credit reports, underwriting fees, processing fees, and wire fees, etc. Along with shopping the source, you will also have to shop the total costs of the loan, including interest rate, broker fees, points (each point is 1% of the amount you borrow), prepayment penalties, loan term, application fees, credit report fee, appraisals, and a host of other items. Just as the car salesperson can sell you that worthless warranty, loan officers and mortgage brokers can rip you off by charging junk fees at the closing table. So the bottom line is . . . check out your mortgage broker. Make a few calls. Be sure to have some references. Look for a company that has been in business for at least three years. There are many very good, honest, up-right mortgage brokers in the business. You just have to work a bit harder to find them.

Which Loan Program?

There isn't a simple answer to the question of "which loan program?" The right type of mortgage for you depends on many different factors:

* your current financial picture
* how you expect your finances to change
* how long you intend to keep your house
* how comfortable you are with your mortgage payment and the possibility of it changing
* how many weeks you intend rent your property
* reasonable rental income potential
* the property's past rental history
* if you intend on "renting by owner" or using a management company to rent (which means you will have to pay commissions)
* if you expect to pay the property off through principal payments or if you are banking on property appreciation to make you money

One rule of thumb to remember is that the more risk for the bank, the more you will have to pay (i.e., higher interest rates and more closing costs).

Term of the Loan

One thing to consider is the term, or length of the loan, and how it will affect your bottom line. For example, a 22-year fixed-rate mortgage instead of a 30-year loan can save you thousands of dollars in interest payments over the life of your loan, but your monthly payments will be higher and make it more difficult for you to break even with your rental income. An adjustable rate mortgage may get you started with a lower monthly payment than a fixed-rate mortgage and may make it easier for your property to pay for itself with your rental income . . . but your payment could increase when the interest rate changes. Get comfortable using one of the many mortgage calculators, available for free online at howtorentbyowner.com. Also try to determine your goals from the day you purchase, and set the term of your loan accordingly.

Before we discuss products, I want you to understand that there are two separate qualification guidelines that must be considered when purchasing each particular product—conforming and non-conforming loans. The products are the same, but the qualification factors are different. A conforming mortgage is just that, the normal, usual way to purchase. Under a conforming mortgage, there are industry-standard, set rules, though the guidelines may still vary from lender to lender. Conforming loans generally require that you fit into the government standards of Fannie Mae and Freddie Mac guidelines***, which may or may not include maximum loan amounts, certain debt-to-income ratios, and minimum credit scores. A non-conforming mortgage is used when you or your property does not fit into that perfect little box. So if you need a huge loan, are self-employed, your credit score is low, or your debt-to-income ratio is high, you may be required to purchase through non-conforming guidelines. Non-conforming loans, as a rule, have an up-charge of 0.75%–1.5% more than conforming loan rates.

***For information on conforming loans figures and facts, visit www.mortgage-x.com.

Second Home or Investment Property?

You need to determine whether you will be using your vacation home as a second home or as an investment property. This makes a big difference in the kind of mortgage you should get. It also has significant income tax implications, but those are separate issue that we won't discuss here (discuss it with your tax adviser). You must

this is only a question for mortgage purchases; how you
property on your income taxes is a completely different
take a look at the different mortgage products available.

Second Home Mortgage

When you go this route, rates are the same as a primary property
mortgage, with minimal down payment. Second mortgages are my
favorite way to purchase a vacation home. There are no "up charges,"
i.e., higher rates (since the bank has very little risk). This is also the type
of loan that the average person is most familiar with. It works exactly
the same way the loan on your primary residence works. Basically, if
you made it through the loan process on your primary residence, then
you can get through the process of a second home mortgage. And for
income tax purposes, you can convert your property from a second
home to an investment property *after* you purchase the loan, which
will maximize all of your income tax deductions. The only caveat is
that you must be able to qualify under the second home's terms. What
does this mean? You have to be able to afford it just as you would
your first home. Under this loan, there is *no consideration for potential
rental income*. So if your primary residence mortgage is $150,000 and
your second home mortgage is $125,000, then you must to be able to
qualify for $275,000 worth of debt. Therefore, if you maxed out your
debt on your primary residence, this is not the type of loan for you.
But have no fear; there are many more options.

Investor Mortgage

This is a mortgage where everyone concerned knows you are buying
the property strictly as an investment. Accordingly, certain factors
come into play. The bank will want to know the rental history of the

property. Also, these types of loans are considered by the lender to be higher risk. So the risk for the bank translates into higher interest rates and higher fees for you.

Fixed-Rate, Fixed-Term

The most commonly used type of mortgage products is fixed-rate mortgages. With these mortgages, your interest rate and monthly payments never change. Property taxes and homeowners' insurance may increase, but your monthly payments will otherwise remain stable.

These mortgages are available for 30 years, 20 years, 15 years, and even 10 years. Under a fixed-rate fully amortizing loan, a large percentage of the monthly payment is used for paying the interest during the early amortization period. As the loan is paid down, more of the monthly payment is applied to principal. A typical 30-year fixed-rate mortgage takes 22.5 years of level payments to pay half of the original loan amount.

Note: Most investment advisors will suggest a loan for an investment property for the longest term. You will have to decide for yourself whether this makes sense for your particular situation.

Adjustable Rate Mortgages (ARM)

These loans generally begin with an interest rate that is 2%–3% below a comparable fixed-rate mortgage and could allow you to buy a more expensive home.

However, the interest rate changes at specified intervals (i.e., every year) depending on changing market conditions. If interest rates go up, your monthly mortgage payment will too. But if rates go down, your mortgage payment will drop.

There are also mortgages that combine aspects of fixed and adjustable rate mortgages starting at a low fixed-rate for 7–10 years, for example, then adjusting to market conditions.

Interest Only Loans (Fixed)

In this case, the borrower gets a very low interest rate, say 3.25%. After 3, 5, 7, or 10 years it automatically converts into a conventional mortgage at 2.5%–3.5% points above the LIBOR rate (As of January 2004, the LIBOR rate was 1.22%. So if you purchased this loan three years ago, it would covert to a fixed-rate loan at 3.72%–4.72%). You only pay the monthly interest amount, and there is no principal payment. With this loan, you build no equity from your payments unless you make additional principal payment. This is a great loan for a property that you are quite certain will appreciate in value over a short period of time.

Interest Only LIBOR Loan

With this loan, you are operating on a floating interest level, which is tied to fluctuating markets. In January 2004, you could obtain a LIBOR loan as low as 2.5%. This type of loan allows you to purchase the most expensive property that you otherwise may never have been able to afford. Take for instance a loan amount of $750,000. With an interest only LIBOR loan, the interest rate may be as low as 2.5%, therefore the payment would be only $1,562 per month as opposed to a 30-year fixed-rate at 5.5%, which would be $4,258 per month. See the difference in how much more you could afford with this type of loan? This is a great product for people that intend on owning for short periods of time and would like to sell or "flip" their property, mostly for the investors who are banking on a huge appreciation.

Of course, this is a more volatile loan and is not for the weak of heart. And buyer beware, because it allows you to afford much more than you could under conventional mortgages, you can easily find yourself way in over your head in debt.

Here are some examples of how payments can differ depending on the product you choose:

Given a mortgage amount of $150,000, a conforming loan with no points or origination fees:

Product	Rate	Payment
30 yr. fixed	5.625%	$863
15 yr. fixed	5.00%	$1,186
1 yr. ARM	3.25%	$653
3/1 ARM	4.0%	$716
5/1 ARM	4.875%	$794
1 yr. interest only LIBOR	2.25%	$281

Portfolio Financing

Did you know that you can use your current stock portfolio to finance a property? Companies such as Merrill Lynch, Payne Webber, and Morgan Stanley now have these products available to property investors. You can use a portion of your portfolio as collateral. What this means is that stock brokerage firms now realize that real estate investment is a viable means of investment. These companies will loan up to three times the amount of your portfolio to purchase real estate. Say you have $100,000 worth of stocks. Your $100,000 stock portfolio would allow you to purchase $300,000 worth of property. Stock brokerage firms even allow you to purchase at 100% financing. So you don't need a down payment, and you don't even have to cash in your stocks! You can still buy, sell, and defer capital gains on liquidated securities and still use pledged securities. Of course, there may be trading restrictions on the collateralized stocks. One thing to remember here is that your mortgage interest may not be deductible if you are using tax-deferred stocks. In some cases, you can pay the principal back according to your own income schedule.

Self-Directed IRA

All of your stocks tied up in your IRAs? Did you know that you can buy real estate, including vacation properties, with your IRA? Jeffrey Desich is a vice president with Equity Trust Company and a registered principal with Mid Ohio Securities. He is actively involved in real estate and the Financial Service Industry, and an expert on real estate investing with self-directed retirement accounts. Here is what he said on the subject:

> With a self-directed IRA, you have the ability to take control of your retirement savings. A self-directed IRA is an Individual Retirement Account in which you call the shots, and you choose your own investments. By investing your IRA in real estate you have the ability to shelter you profits from taxes! Both rental income and appreciation of the property grows either tax-deferred or tax-free!
>
> With these self-directed accounts you have the ability to invest in stocks, bonds, mutual funds, and special assets, such as vacation properties. If you choose to use your IRA to purchase property, you must select a custodian for your self-directed IRA. When selecting a custodian for your self-directed IRA, you want to make sure you ask a few questions:
>
> + Does this custodian offer one low flat fee with no hidden costs?
> + Am I allowed to invest in non-traditional assets like vacation properties?

+ Does the custodian have experience and knowledge in real estate?
+ Is the firm federally regulated?
+ Will I have the ability to speak with knowledgeable individuals and not just an automated service?

Once your IRA owns the property, all expenses related to this investment will be paid from the funds in your self-directed IRA, per your direction. In addition, all income made from the investment will be sent into your IRA, where it grows tax-deferred or tax-free depending on the account type.

Note: This loan also has strict government guidelines.

Down Payments

Let's face it. Coming up with the down payment is the most common problem of homebuyers. If everybody had 20% cash to put down, things would be simple. But this is the real world. This is where, through creative financing, most of the obstacles to acquiring the necessary down payment can be overcome. Remember the days when the banks probed into the source of your down payment and borrowing a down payment was taboo? Well, no longer. Now the banks not only allow it, they have products specifically set-up for that purpose.

First, you should understand that basically all loans *over the 80% loan-to-value range* will require PMI, which is private mortgage insurance. This is expensive and can only be deducted for income tax purposes under certain investment property guidelines. Be sure to check with your accountant or CPA prior to purchasing the loan to see if he or she thinks that you will be able to deduct PMI. If you cannot deduct it, then you have to put down the 20% down payment to avoid it, right? Nope! You can borrow it.

Mortgage brokers have yet another product that you can consider. They are called piggyback loans or 80/10/10 or 80/15/5 loans. Let's first look at the 80/15/5 loan. In this case, you acquire a first mortgage for 80% loan to value, a simultaneous second mortgage for 15%, and are required to have a 5% down payment. The same applies for the 80/10/10 where your first mortgage is 80%, you get a second mortgage of 10%, and you must come up with the 10% down payment. While the second mortgage will have a higher interest rate than your first mortgage, the elimination of the PMI insurance generally covers that difference. Here, while all of the interest can be deducted for tax purposes, the PMI cannot and is virtually money thrown out the window.

Let's fast forward. You're ready to buy. What is the best way to approach the seller? Well, there are a couple of ways. On the one hand you can be pre-qualified for a loan, but even better is to come to the table armed with a pre-approval letter. Here is the difference between the two:

Pre-Qualification

In this case, you go to the loan officer and tell him or her your income and expenses. He or she will punch in a few numbers, maybe run a quick credit report, and then tell you how much you can afford. This is just a verbal approximation and comes with no guarantees that you will qualify for the loan.

While a pre-qualification can help you approximate how much you can afford, it does not offer the same advantages as being pre-approved.

Pre-Approved Pending Property

In the case of a pre-approved loan, you have not only gone to the loan officer for pre-qualification, he or she has actually sent your file to processing and underwriting, and you are completely approved for a specific loan amount. With this product, the lender is just waiting for the sales contract and property to fill in the blanks on the closing documents. Pre-approval pending property is like having a blank check-in your pocket just waiting to be filled out! Why do this? It gives you leverage as a buyer.

Realize that vacation homes and investment properties can be located in two significantly different markets. Seller's markets or buyer's markets. Take for instance Cape Cod, a well-known seller's market. Cape Cod has been developed for nearly 300 years; there's no more land to be had. So each time a property goes up for sale there may 10 or more buyers fighting to purchase it. If you were the seller, which offer would you accept? Sell to the person who does not have a loan yet, and take the risk that that buyer will not qualify for the loan? Or, would you sell to the buyer who has already gone through whole mortgage process and has full loan approval? Of course you would pick the sure deal.

Then there is the other type of vacation property market, the buyer's markets, where there are several dozen, maybe even hundreds of properties for buyers to choose from. In a buyer's market, homes may be on the market for longer periods of time. As the savvy buyer with your pre-approval in your pocket, you can go to the seller and offer considerably less than the asking price and have a better chance of the seller accepting your offer. This is the way I purchased our first property in Destin, Florida, back in the 1990s. I got pre-approved for a loan. I went and looked at numerous properties priced within my pre-approval dollar amount. I then narrowed my choices down to 10 properties. My plan was to give low-ball offers and keep going down the line until I found a seller who would take my offer. I put an offer on the first property and told the sellers that I could close in two weeks! Back then, two weeks was unheard of for closing. Most mortgages took four to six weeks to process. The sellers were not as offended as my realtor thought they might be. The property had been on the market for more than six months, and they had already had two contracts fall through due to buyers not being able to qualify for the loan. So the sellers made a counter offer, and I agreed to split the difference. I called the appraiser and inspector, asked if they could have the property ready to close in a week, and they went along with it. In the end, I purchased the property at 86% of the market value and closed in one week! I started off with 14% equity in the property from day one! That's pretty tough to beat (but I want you to try).

The bottom line when it comes to mortgages is . . . learn how to be a wise consumer. Again, the car analogy is appropriate. When was the last time you paid the sticker price or test drove only one car? It just doesn't work that way. You did a lot of shopping around before signing on the dotted line. Well mortgages are a much bigger purchase than an automobile, and there is so much more at stake. Don't be afraid to ask questions. Kick the tires, check with previous customers, and do a good deal of comparison-shopping. Chances are there is an excellent mortgage product available that will specifically address your situation and your needs. But it won't leap into your arms. It's up to you to go out there and find it.

3

Crunch the Numbers

Every vacation homeowner has to determine his or her break-even point. This is the point where your income to date from the property meets the expenses projected for the entire year. This will determine whether you will be making a profit or a loss.

Let me explain why this is so important. One of the goals when you purchased your vacation home, of course, was to achieve a break-even cash flow (on a year-to-year basis), coupled with a maximum tax shelter on other earned income. My definition of the break-even point is when all the income (rent) from your property is enough to pay all of the bills associated with ownership of the property. In other words, your property should not cost you another dime after your down payment. Now, that's not necessarily the definition you will get from financial analysts. Let's face it, they talk in ways that most of us cannot understand. They would say that break-even is a point at which your income is equal to the initial investment with all factors included, such as investments, depreciation, tax benefits, losses, and liabilities. The total revenue for your small business. They use terms like: total direct expenses incurred, revenues minus direct expense, contribution rate of contribution per unit of revenue, total fixed establishment expenses, and so on.

I am not an accountant and chances are, neither are you, so we'll talk in terms that you and I can understand and not worry about the things that your accountant will take into consideration when he or she handles your income taxes.

Now, I said your property should not cost you another dime after your down payment. You're probably asking, is that realistic? Absolutely! Let me show you how. Here's my formula: if your monthly mortgage payment is less than or equal to one peak week rental, and you rent approximately 17 weeks per year, you will indeed break even. Here's how:

- Peak weeks—the highest earning weeks of the rental season. Usually there are 12 peak weeks in a rental year. So if you rent these 12 weeks, you will have enough revenue to pay your mortgage payments for the entire year.
- Roughly, your mortgage payments (including taxes and insurance) should be equal to, or less than, one peak week's earnings.
- Other costs, including bills for your phone, power, cable, and association dues, are paid by your earnings from approximately five off-week rentals. So, even by renting only 17 weeks out of the year, you can still break even. These other costs, as you can see, are also paid for.

This formula is not absolute, of course, but it will at least give you a good feel for the numbers.

It would be nice if we had control over everything, including our financial lives. But, of course, that is not how things work in the real world. Certain things you can influence, others you can't. First, let's take a look at what you *can* do to help increase the value of your vacation home.

The most obvious way is by making improvements to your property. Consider not only improvements that make your vacation home more aesthetically pleasing, such as new paint or wallpaper, but also upgrades that expand the enjoyment potential of the vacation home. Upgrades include items such as a hot tub, a beach side spigot to wash away sand, a ski boot drying rack, cable TV, a barbecue set-up, etc. Think of the various things you might enjoy if you were a renter. The list is almost endless.

There are also certain factors that you *can't* control that nonetheless affect your property's appreciation. But even though you have no influence over these things, you should still be aware of them, and how they can help you. A good example would be improvements that are provided with the aid of a tourist development tax. This tax is added to state sales tax in many places in order to improve the tourist potential of the area. A typical sales tax add-on would be 3%. For this, the state can offer a variety of area improvements to piers, beaches, and things like providing shuttle service to the beach, tourist viewing areas, etc.

Other appreciation factors that we owners can't influence include economic ups and downs and the rise and fall of interest rates. Yet, you still need to be well aware of these things, and keep yourself informed. A knowledgeable owner is more likely to become a wealthy owner.

And, speaking of knowledge, please don't overlook the importance of understanding the crucial subject of insurance. First, you need to realize that there are many different types of insurance. If your home or condo is in an association, sometimes they have a master insurance policy. With this kind of policy, the common grounds are covered under a blanket policy. It will insure the exterior walls of the building, generally up to the sheet rock. If your building is covered by such a policy, you will probably not be required to purchase separate insurance. Still, in my opinion, I think you should. Otherwise, you do not have coverage for everything *inside* your property, such as cabinets, fixtures, or just about anything else of value.

You also need to consider extra insurance if your property is located in certain areas where you may be at high risk for natural disasters, such as hurricanes or floods. The property's proximity to the ocean or lakes will obviously affect your risk. Yes, this extra coverage can get expensive, so you will need to carefully look into it. For example, when I was looking for a new property, I considered a place that was directly on the beach. The hurricane insurance was $3,600 per year! However, a property right across the street was only $600 per year. So be sure to do your homework.

Another type of insurance you may want to consider is personal liability insurance. You can select this option as a rider policy on your current homeowner's insurance as an extension of liability on your second home. This is important because, in our overly litigious society, what happens if someone slips and hurts themselves in your shower, then decides it's your fault? You get the idea. Protect yourself.

There is also a specialized kind of policy known as rental insurance. This covers you in case you have a loss of rental income revenue due to things such as floods, fires, etc. The cost, in my opinion, is too high to justify, and I personally don't carry it. You may be different, however, and feel more secure covering every possibility. That is a decision you will have to make for yourself.

If you choose a condominium for your vacation home, please realize that there will almost certainly be a condo fee. These are assessed monthly, quarterly, or bi-annually. This is to fund the operations of the association and a board of officers who are elected from the ownership to direct the operations either directly or through a hired property manager. Don't let the condo fee scare you away. There are many benefits to purchasing a condo (discussed in the next chapter). This chapter has been mostly about the numbers, but never forget, owning a vacation home can also be a lot of fun. Who can put a price on that?

CHAPTER

4

Buying the Right Place
· · · For You

We're now at the point where you've made certain critical decisions. You have carefully analyzed your personal situation, you've crunched the numbers, and you've decided that buying a vacation property does indeed make sense for you. Now what? How exactly do you go about the process of buying the right place for you? The choices you make at this stage of the game will impact your finances and lifestyle for many years to come.

Let's start by eliminating the "don't wanters," those aspects of a vacation property that you don't want, under any circumstances. First, you do not want to purchase a home where there are laws or restrictions prohibiting short-term or transient rentals. Check the local laws and neighborhood or complex rules. Condominium complexes are notorious for having exclusive in-house rental management companies which would prohibit you from renting by owner—if your objective is to cash flow on your property, I would stay away from these types of properties. Some municipalities have very strict guidelines as to when you can and cannot rent, some do not allow rentals at all. Properties on government owned land, such as Army Corp of Engineers, or state and nationally protected lands often carry very strict rules also. This is where a licensed local real estate agent would most likely be a valuable source for information.

As for the structure itself, I would not recommend you purchase a property that requires a lot of maintenance. Even if you are the handyman type, this new venture will be quite different than fixing things up around your own residence once in a while. It's not just a quick trip to the local home improvement mega store to pick up a new storm door or a washer for that pesky leaky kitchen faucet. No, if you buy a high maintenance house, costly repairs will require frequent attention. And here's the key—you'll be doing it *at a distance*. Chances are, your vacation property is not going to be right up the street from where you live (otherwise, going there wouldn't be much of a vacation!). So every time the vacation home needs maintenance, you will have to get in the car and make a long drive, arriving worn and tired before you even begin the work. The alternative—hiring workers to do the job—can be quite expensive. And, you won't be there to supervise the work they do and to make sure they don't run up the bill. Not a good idea. There's a good deal of truth in the old adage: "If you want something done right, do it yourself." But it can be rather difficult when you live 300 miles away.

The solution? Buy a low-maintenance property. I know that sounds incredibly simple, but you might be surprised at how easy it can be to overlook things that should be obvious. After all, this is probably something you've never done before, and nothing is ever simple until you have some experience with it. The best way to find out the condition of a house is by employing a home inspector. It's always money well spent. Of particular interest in the home inspector's report will be the condition of the roof, electrical wiring, heating system, and the plumbing. These are all non-cosmetic items that often are not readily apparent to the naked eye. But they are some of the major areas of a house that tend to erode with time, and repairing them can be expensive and time consuming. Buy a home without these problems to begin with, and you will save yourself many days of headaches in the years ahead.

Here's another consideration to take into account. Many people think it's a great bargain to do the exact opposite of what I've just said. They intentionally buy a house with many problems because the price will be lower. Then, they rehab this diamond in the rough and end up with a lavish home for a cheap price. While that may sound good in theory, and there certainly are cases where people have made money this way, doing a successful rehab is much more difficult than most people imagine. Did you ever see the movie *The Money Pit?* It may be a Hollywood comedy, and an exaggeration, but it also contains a valuable lesson. Just like when the government makes an estimate on a public works project, when the final numbers are added up, it inevitably seems that the project comes in over budget rather than under. The same tends to be true when you try to rehab a house with a number of repair issues. Moreover, during the period that you are making your repairs you will not be able to rent it out. Your cash flow will be put on hold indefinitely. I'm not ruling the idea out completely, but carefully consider these potential problems before going the rehab route.

This is why I personally love condominiums. For starters, maintenance is much easier. There is no roof to repair, no lawn to mow (you probably do enough of that at your residence!), no snow to shovel, and no leaves to rake. Do you see my point? Moreover, a condominium complex, in all likelihood, will include a bunch of nice extras that you probably won't get in a single family dwelling, such as Olympic-size pools, hot tubs, golf courses, health clubs, and more.

And one of the best advantages of condos is that they usually are situated in the very best locations—right on the beach, right next to that big ski mountain, or directly on the lake. Developers know all of the ideal spots to buy up real estate, and they always manage to get their hands on the most coveted land and turn it into something beautiful.

Here's what real estate pro Jack Simpson said on the subject: "You should always consider the view value of a property before buying. Maybe view isn't the only thing to you personally, or perhaps you aren't even going to live there. But, you should still consider view. Properties with a good view will rent better and be worth more when it's time to sell."

Good words of advice. Get out there and start searching. I'm betting you can find a condo with a great view, which will make it that much more valuable.

Now the downside. Some condo associations limit the use of the property. For example, in some beach towns, you may be required to occupy the premises yourself for a certain number of weeks per year. This means, of course, that you can't rent as much as you want. They can also impose various rules about renting, such as age restrictions, and "quiet times." They can sometimes charge "special assessments" that you would never have to pay with a single-family home.

Still, when you look at the big picture, I think the benefits of condo ownership outweigh the drawbacks. They may not be the perfect solution for a vacation home, but I think purchasing a vacation condo will be a decision you won't regret.

Another area that you need to explore before making your final decision about a purchase is the question: do you build (buy pre-construction) or buy home that is already built? There is a whole set of factors to consider. First, you need to realize that, in most cases, buying pre-construction can be more expensive up front. You usually have to come up with a larger down payment. Also, you have to buy all of the furnishings. This is in sharp contrast to purchasing a vacation home that has already been built, as these homes typically are sold fully furnished. Not only does buying the furnishings mean paying additional money, it also means additional work. Be prepared to spend a good deal of time cruising furniture stores, looking for sales, making sure what you want is in stock, setting up delivery dates, and handling a number of other hassles. On the other hand, you won't have to worry about buying a place that you love that comes with a set of furniture that you hate!

Now, I should also mention that although buying a pre-construction home can be expensive initially, in the long run you might be better off financially. The reason is, appreciation. In all likelihood, you will see better appreciation in your first three years of ownership with a pre-construction. This is because of the delay between the day you purchase a pre-construction and the day it is actually built. Typically, that can be three years for a condo and one year for a house. The builder needs to sell at a reduced price so he or she can get the project off the ground, so he or she sells pre-constructions at a reduced rate, which later works to your benefit in the form of accelerated appreciation in the years immediately following your purchase.

For a more detailed look at just how this process works, read what Jack Simpson, owner of Holiday Isle Properties, a real estate company, said in a recent article: "First, the developer acquires the land and applies for a construction loan. To reduce risk, lenders typically require the developer to sell at least half of the condo units with a binding contract before funding the construction loan. Since it is harder to sell sky and paper than something that you can actually see and feel, the developer discounts the purchase price to achieve the required pre-sales. Pre-sales are usually done first on a non-binding reservation agreement with a few thousand dollars as a good faith deposit. This is called the reservation stage. Buyers can opt out anytime in this stage and receive a full refund.

After the lender-required units are reserved, the developer delivers the final condominium documents to the buyers. These documents describe the condominium project in great detail. This is called the contract stage. Buyers then have 15 days to look over the documents and decide whether to "go hard on the contract" or to back out and have their reservation deposits refunded. Going hard on the contract normally requires buyers to make an additional deposit, which combined with the reservation fee, will be 20% of the purchase price. At hard contract stage, the deposit becomes non-refundable. Some fallout may occur as the result of a few buyers opting out. With the required number of firm contracts in hand, the developer has the construction loan funded and building begins. Buyers do not close and start making payments until the project is completed with a certificate of occupancy."

Like so many other aspects of business, when it comes to deciding exactly when to purchase your vacation home, timing is everything. Please don't waste your money by making your purchase at the wrong time. And when would that be? At the height of the rental season. That may not have been the answer you expected, but there is a good reason for it. That is the time when there are the fewest available vacation homes for sale, which makes it a seller's market. As the buyer, it's not a good deal for you. The opposite, of course, is true during the off-season. At that time there are many more available vacation homes for sale to choose from, which tends to lower prices and create more of a buyer's market.

Another reason why buying during the off-season makes sense will become clear to you when you become more familiar with how the vacation rental cycle works. Most renters book their vacations 60 to 90 days ahead of time. So if you buy in February, for example (the middle of the off-season in most U.S. locations), you will be in an excellent position to lock in renters for May and beyond. By contrast, if you made the mistake of buying during the peak of the season (let's say July) by the time you were ready to start accepting new renters you would have already missed out on some of the prime months for vacationers. That would mean more of the expenses right up front would have to be paid out of your pocket rather than by the renters. See why timing is so important?

When you're finally ready to buy, the critical issue of price rises to the forefront. First, let me ease any fears that you may have that you are buying during a so-called real estate bubble. This is when the prices are high, perhaps artificially so, and many buyers are worried that they will get soaked when the bubble bursts. That would only be true if you were going into this for a quick turnaround. But our discussion is about buying for the long haul. And, so long as you can rent out the property and generate revenue from it, the property will pay for itself. In other words, the cash flow from the renters will make you impervious to even cataclysmic fluctuations in real estate prices. So if you plan on buying this vacation property and keeping it for a considerable amount of time, you have absolutely nothing to fear from the dreaded bubble.

The best position to be in is to be pre-approved for a mortgage (in writing) before you pick up the phone and talk to the first real estate broker. This can, in many cases, put you in the driver's seat, setting the stage for buying a vacation home significantly below its market value. When you are pre-approved, you are automatically much more attractive to sellers. It all depends, of course, on the market conditions. In a tight market, the sellers are more likely to get their asking price, or close to it. So you have to know how to adapt your bids to changing conditions (much the way you would with the stock market). If it is a buyer's market, not only should you not accept the asking price, you should go for a much lower price.

Many people are afraid or intimidated to bid lower than the asking price. Don't be. No one is going to be offended. This isn't personal (it's not, "I think your house is lousy, and I'm not going to pay only this much for it"). This is a business transaction. You don't know the sellers' circumstances. They might be going through a divorce, bankruptcy, or some other hardship and are desperate to sell. Your significantly lower bid might be perfectly acceptable to them. Besides, you have nothing to lose by trying. The worst they can say is "No," usually with a counter-offer, and then you can continue to negotiate. There is no reason in the world why you shouldn't try to get the best possible deal for yourself.

There are other ways to save money too. Check with your tax advisor about the tax advantages you may have by owning a vacation home. Did you consider all of the deductions you will be entitled to? Not only is there the depreciation on your property that can be deducted every year, but also maintenance of the property is deductible. That includes the cost of trips that you make to your vacation home for the purpose of anything pertaining to your rental of it. That could include trips to show it to prospective renters, do maintenance, or any other legitimate reason. Do the math. All of that adds up, and your tax bill happily shrinks as a result.

Let me share a few case studies with you to give you a better understanding of some of the different scenarios we've been discussing. All of these stories are true, but the names have been changed for privacy reasons.

> Lauren bought a two-bedroom, two-bath pre-construction, beachfront condo in Florida. She bought during the pre-sale stage. The purchase price at pre-sale was $195,000. At the time of hard contract, she had to put down 20% of the purchase price; she put 10% down ($19,500) and had a secured letter of credit for the remainder of the 20% deposit. The construction took three years to complete. Lauren closed on the property the day it was built and sold it two hours later for $325,000. So her initial cash investment of $19,500 became $130,000 . . . earning her $110,500 in three years! That's an annualized return of 88.20% and a return for the entire three year period of 566.59%.

Here's another story that I think you will find informative.

Gabe bought the same two-bedroom, two-bath home as Lauren, at the same price, and at the same time. He chose to furnish his unit and rent it (furnishings cost him $16,000). In the first year, his rentals were slow and sparse, and he had to pay out $5,000 out-of-pocket to pay the mortgage and expenses. The second year he had better rental business and just barely managed break-even cash flow, having to pay $1,000 out-of-pocket. He sold his unit, after two years of renting, for $400,000. Coupled with the two years of rental loss and the cost to furnish the property, it cost him around $22,000 in extra cash investment. Now, let's break down precisely what happened. Gabe invested a total of $41,500 (down payment + furnishings + negative cash flow for the first two years) over five years, and it became $164,500! That's an annualized return of 52.61% and a return for the entire five-year period of 727.78%!

While these numbers are certainly high and are best-case scenarios, these kinds of investments really do exist in the marketplace. You just have to do some research to find them.

Here's another example.

Ashley purchased an existing, furnished beachfront condo for $165,000 in 1999. She put down $8,250. She had positive cash flow from day one, earning $23,000 (above and beyond all the expenses) over the five-year period. She earned $2,000 the first year, $3,500 the second year, $4,100 the third year, $6,000 the fourth year, and $7,400 the last year. In 2003, she sold the condo for $300,000. That's an annualized return of 40.58%, with return for the entire period of 449.06%.

Let me show you yet another perspective. I spoke with Sean, who co-owns a cabin with his two siblings in Illinois. The three siblings live in different areas all over the country. In 1996, they had an interesting idea. Their father owned and lives on a beautiful 100-acre property (the family homestead). They wanted to build a cabin that all three could use. Their initial intent was to build a place that they could use for large family gatherings. Although they did not need to make the initial investment for the land, they still incurred building and furnishing costs. They decided that the best way to offset those cost was to rent out their cabin part of the time. Being in an obscure area with no real tourism and no option to use a management company, they decided to rent their cabin themselves (by owner). They were not sure how successful they would be but figured any amount, even small, could help offset their costs and still enable them to use the property themselves. Well, they put their property on the Internet, and low and behold, people wanted to rent it. Their property rents mostly on weekends, and they rent a few full weeks per year. This family found that the rentals not only paid for their bank note but also allows them some extra income to upgrade (hot tub, swing set, etc.) and maintain their cabin. For maintenance, they get together at least one week per year at their cabin. During that week, they designate one workday. Sean said, "We all pitch in and work together to accomplish our deep clean and maintenance list." Naturally, they are very pleased with their decision to build and rent their cabin.

OK, here's another example of some folks who purchased their vacation house for self use and are renting it out to help pay for it.

Zachary and his wife own property in a popular Colorado ski resort. They purchased it 15 years ago. They live two hours away. They rent it 10–16 weeks per year but use their property a whopping 60 nights a year themselves! They are very selective about their renters and actually turn down rentals. They strictly rent only to offset the costs for personal use. They find most of their renters through the Internet, but also find the local ski magazines/brochures a useful advertising tool. They have found that renting in a ski area, all of their renters expect a hot tub. Zachary is a member of the condominium board, and he pushed for the complex to build a hot tub on the premises. They stated that this was a very wise investment for the complex. And now it has one.

One last note about your adventure in buying: you don't have to do it alone. You may initially think that if you work directly with the seller, cutting out the middleman, you will save money. Well, maybe. Or maybe not. Especially if you are buying in an area you are not familiar with, there are so many things a qualified professional realtor can help you with. For example, if you are buying in a different state, often the laws governing real estate are different than the laws in your home state. You need someone who is thoroughly familiar with the area and its vacation scene, someone who can readily answer the dozens of questions you're likely to have. One place to start researching vacation areas and to find qualified real estate professionals is www.EscapeHomes.com. Of course, don't become completely reliant on this person. Make sure you do your homework each step of the way. After all, you're the one who will be signing all of those papers at closing. And you're the one who will be enjoying your wonderful new vacation home for years to come. Happy hunting!

CHAPTER

5

Why Self-Management Makes Sense

Well, congratulations. You own it! You finally made the big decision to follow your dream and buy that vacation home. So ... now what? You want the property to start generating cash right away, but you want to be careful to do everything right. Let's start with the basics. You have three choices.

1. You can hire a management company to handle everything.
2. You can use a management partnership program.
3. You can self-manage ... as in "rent by owner."

Option number three, rent by owner, is the only way to maximize your income on your vacation property. In other words, it's your best bet. Of course, this depends on how much work you are willing to do. But I'm not talking about backbreaking work, or even a huge commitment of time. Remember the old adage, its not how *hard* you work, it's how *smart* you work. That is certainly solid advice when it comes to renting your property on your own. So don't be scared into thinking it's a Herculean task. It's not.

I know what you're thinking at this point: is it really worth it to do it myself? Yes! Here's why. From my experience, I have discovered two main reasons to rent by owner. The first is the more obvious reason. You guessed it . . . it's money. You can net more money simply by not paying management company commissions, which may be significantly higher than you realize. Then, there are savings on things such as linen-pools, credit card fees, and cleaning fees (when you rent by owner, you charge the cleaning fee on top of the regular rental rate and taxes). The second reason will surprise you because it seems to be everyone's biggest worry: having complete control of who rents your unit. I like to talk to each renter on the phone. This is my chance to get to know these folks. I am friendly and personable and let the renters know that they are renting my second home. This is a great way to build a rapport. And, by establishing this relationship, the renters now change from customers to friends. Friends will take care of your unit. If you stay in a hotel and spill coffee on the carpet, what do you do? Probably nothing. But if you rent a friend's place, how differently would you handle that spilled coffee? My renters take care of my unit, and so will yours.

This really goes further than the obvious. Let's face it. There are certain categories of people you will no doubt *not* want to rent to. I'm not by any means talking about racial, ethnic, or religious distinctions. But a bunch of rowdy, hard-drinking college spring breakers are almost sure to do some damage. They are all but guaranteed to be partying and carousing. Just imagine how many things could be broken. What a hassle they might cause for the neighbors. Who wants to negotiate with college students about recovering damages? You can almost guess how that's going to turn out (and it's not a pretty picture for you). You, as the owner, have the ability (and a duty to yourself) to speak with each renter. Proper screening will help you weed out these types of renters. Refer to Chapter 11 for tips on how to weed out less desirable renters.

Another major fear for owners managing their properties themselves is maintenance. You are probably asking questions like, what do I do if the air conditioning goes out? What if the toilet stops up? What if the renters lose their keys? The simple truth is . . . these things rarely happen. Don't let these issues make you run into the arms of a management company! These are all things that we will discuss in detail later in the book. One thing to keep in mind is that when a renter calls the management company, the management company most likely has to contract a repairman. You can just as easily call the repairman from your home 600 miles away. So don't make your decision based on this alone.

Another good reason to rent by owner is you *will control the vacancies.* No matter what management companies say, *your best interests are not their first concern.* Remember, they may have 100 customers (owners) to worry about. You only have one—yourself. For example, management companies will sometimes sell a mid-week rental leaving very valuable, easy-to-rent days open. What the company is doing is taking the easy way out. But the easy way is not always the best way (at least not for you). However, if you make yourself dependent on these middlemen, you will have no choice. You see, a management company looks at it this way: let's say the company has a 100 rental units that it manages. What does the company do if it gets 100 qualified renters? Does the company try to match the renters' needs to the right properties for the right dates, regardless of which properties get the most bookings? Actually, the answer is no. If the company did it that way, certain owners would end up with a disproportionate amount of bookings, and the management company would have a few very happy owners and many unhappy owners. And, of course, unhappy owners will not renew their contracts, and the management company will lose money. So the company spreads the qualified renters around, making sure all of the owners receive at least some rentals. You can bet that company will try its hardest to make sure each unit gets one week booked . . . it's all about keeping volume and revenue going. From the company's perspective, it's better to have 100 semi-happy owners rather than a bunch that are fuming mad when they end up with zero bookings. What you need to realize, of course, is that what is in the company's best interest, in many cases, is diametrically opposed to what is in your best interest.

Renting by owner allows you to break free from this far from ideal situation. Here is an example of an owner who, without a management company, took advantage of filling his vacancies to the fullest:

Fred owned a property on Cape Cod for 20 years. When he retired from his job, he did a little research and decided to take on the task of renting by owner. He thought it would be fun to do. Fred's cottage always rented very well during the peak season. On the Cape, that is June through August. But he never had any off-season rentals. Then, he advertised his property on the Internet. He not only filled up the peak season, he also rented many off weeks and long weekends during the fall, winter, and spring. He nearly doubled his rental occupancy from 8–10 weeks when using the management company, to 16–18 weeks on his own. He is now helping out a couple of other owners by booking their properties for them.

Another benefit of self-management is that you can better control your personal use of the property. Many times, management companies make you sign a contract stating you will allow the company to rent a certain number of weeks. The company may even dictate when you can use your own property, for instance, the company may not want you to occupy the property during Christmas, spring break, or the Fourth of July. These are often the highest revenue weeks, and the company does not want owners using those weeks themselves. As a self-manager, you set aside the time you want for vacation or some special event. After all, what good is owning the place if you don't retain control over when you get to enjoy your own property?

Renting by owner is the best way to achieve a positive cash flow. Remember how we talked about break-even point back in Chapter 3? Let's plug in some real numbers and look at this formula as a rent by owner. Remember, if your monthly mortgage payment is equal to or less than one peak week rental rate, then you should be able to achieve positive cash flow. Here's how: take a property that rents for $1,000 a week during peak season with a monthly mortgage payment of $1,000. There are 12 peak weeks (Memorial Day to the third week in August), most if not all of which are generally going to be occupied. If you rent these 12 peak weeks, then you have just made enough money to pay one whole year's mortgage payments. Then you'll need to rent five more weeks to pay for incidentals like power, phone, association dues, minor maintenance, etc. Rent by owner and have 17 weeks booked (33% occupancy), and you have break-even cash flow. Rent more and you have positive cash flow.

And while we're talking about money, when you rent yourself, you are accepting all the payments yourself. So guess *where* the renters are sending those payments? Right to you! You get all *your* money up front. Management companies don't send you your money until 30 days after month end. Some companies don't send out the money until it has cleared the credit card companies, which can take up to 90 days.

Carol, a client of mine, called me on February 1. She called me to thank me for the seminar that she attended a few months prior. Carol was especially excited to report that she had booked her whole summer already. She had 15 weeks booked at $1,000 per week. She required her renters to send a $200 deposit and the full rent upfront. She had $18,000 worth of rental money in her bank account already. She brought up a good point: Think about this . . . the management

he used prior to "renting by owner" managed over 100
latively small management company). If the company
)0 properties then they would have $1.8 million in the
terest for four to six months. When was the last time
interest check on *your* money that the management
ling?

Using a Management Company

Because they offer convenience, there is, of course, a strong appeal to
using a management company. But it's not worth it. And don't let a
realtor try to convince you otherwise. The majority of realtors in vacation property areas are also property managers, so when they make
their case they are doing much more than trying to help you. They are
going to try to convince you that they can rent your property better
than you can. I'm betting that they can't.

Now, let's look at our break-even formula when using a management company. For the sake of argument, let's just say you rent the
same number of weeks, 12 peak and 5 other weeks, and your rental
rate is the same. For every week you rent, management companies take
30% for commissions (usually more, but I'll be conservative). So now
your $1,000 becomes $700. Then the management company charges
you a cleaning fee of $50 ("by owners" charge the renter). Now your
$700 becomes $650. If your renters use a credit card you get charged
a 2% fee. American Express is even more. So your $650 becomes
$630. With these charges alone, you have just given away 37% of your
money. Therefore, you would need to book 27 weeks (52% occupancy)
to equal the same amount of net cash in your pocket as the person
who rents by owner. What I'm saying here is that you will need to
rent 10 more weeks with a management company to come up with the
same money. Math doesn't lie.

Truly, the example above is a very conservative figure. If you currently use a management company, you are probably shaking your head and saying, "No way." Besides the commissions, add the other incidental charges and fees then you'll see that the figure that the management companies' keep becomes more like 50%–60% of your gross profit.

All of this begs the question, why then, would anyone use a management company? Because they're afraid of what they perceive as the risks of renting by owner. For example, my biggest fear, the phone call I fervently hate to receive, is that a renter has arrived, and the unit has not been cleaned. My cleaning service is definitely my lifeline. Using a reliable service is crucial. I wish I had a magical solution to this problem, but it is by far the most difficult part of renting by owner. (It is not insurmountable, however, and we'll talk about how this can be avoided in a later chapter.)

I get the feeling that some of you are still not convinced. You're thinking, I have a family and work full-time. How much time will doing it myself take on a daily basis? This is a realistic question. You *must* have some extra time, because there is indeed work involved. Here's how my time is spent. Throughout the year, I usually spend 5–15 minutes per day responding to email and voice inquiries. My busiest time (for Florida rentals) is from January to March 31, when I may spend an hour or so emailing and calling. This is when I make 80% of the bookings for the whole season. After I'm booked (which is generally by April 1), I spend approximately one half hour per week sending directions and mailing deposit refunds. Four times a year I spend 30 minutes filling out my sales tax forms, and I do have to visit at least twice a year. Oh, I almost forgot, you also have to factor in one to two trips per week to cash the rental checks. But that's a happy chore.

And don't ever fool yourself into thinking that everything will be coming up roses if you just sit back and let the management company do all of the work. After all, you say, how much money could it cost me?

Here's a horror story of one woman who purchased her dream vacation home and rented through a management company.

Karen bought her dream vacation property in Destin, Florida. She is a very business savvy individual and really did her research. Her objective was to purchase a property that she could use herself and rent out when she was not there. When researching properties, she not only factored in the price of the property, she also took into consideration the cost of ownership. Karen used her computer; she opened a spreadsheet, and went through all the numbers. She factored in 30%–40% for management company commissions as a cost of ownership, and surmised that she could afford to purchase the property, even with those commissions. She accepted the fact that it would cost her some money out-of-pocket on an annual basis and was quite happy with the numbers.

Well, even though Karen did her homework, that's not exactly how it worked out. Here's what really happened. . . . Karen bought her dream home and contracted a management company to rent and manage the property for her. She went through the main rental season and did not receive her moneys in a timely fashion from her management company. So from day one, they were taking money out of her pocket. When she finally received her first invoice and rental check, she was astonished to find out that the management company took 83% of her rental revenue! No, your eyes didn't deceive you . . . 83%!

Don't believe it? Neither did I. Karen showed me her invoice. Here's how she got gypped out of her money. The management company rented her place for two- and three-night rentals. (Even though it was peak season when they very easily could have filled full weeks.) So, in a given month where her rental revenue was $4,000, she received a check for $680. Here's how the management company broke it down: in the month there were 31 days, the company had every night occupied at $130 per night. There were nine two-night rentals, three three-night rentals, and one four-night rental. The unit had to be cleaned 14 times. The management company required that the owner pay for cleanings, so 14 cleanings multiplied by $75 is $1,050. Then, the management company assessed a linen refresh fee of $350 (the company said this was a standard fee to all owners mid-season). There was a $120 charge for credit card fees and an $80 fee for beach chair rental (the management company ran a special for "free" beach service on the four-day rental, and charged the owner for the expense!) Then the company charged her $25 for the furnace filter to be changed, and $8 for each of three light bulbs changed. $500 to replace a TV that was missing (why wasn't the renter charged?), $150 for carpet cleaning, $75 for pest control (even though the complex did it regularly as part of the association dues), $75 for an after hours call for a lost key, and $71 for a maintenance call on a clogged garbage disposal. Finally, adding insult to injury, was the most ridiculous fee I had ever heard of . . . they kept $800 of the rental income in an escrow account. For what? Karen never did get an answer to this one.

In the end, Karen faced having to sell her property at a loss—even though it had appreciated 20% in the last year. Now, don't be discouraged. Her comeback story is truly amazing. She consulted with me, fired her management company, and after nine months of self-management she earned $28,000 in rental income, all of which she kept. Three years later Karen has purchased three more properties and is self managing all of them!

Partnership Programs

For those of you who were wondering, there *is* a compromise between hiring a management company and doing all of the work yourself. It is called a partnership program. This is when you agree to have a management company manage your property . . . but only part of the time. How do you find out about these programs? Seize the initiative by going directly to the management company and offering them a deal . . . if I book, then I'll give you X, and if *you* book, I'll pay you X. But what's a reasonable commission? Usually what you should offer is 10%–15% off the company's regular commission rates. This is business that they would not get otherwise. While it's not ideal, you'll be surprised by how open they will be to your suggestions. And, there is a lot of room to negotiate, such as which weeks they will handle management issues, just the weeks they have the place booked or all of the time? These finer points of the partnership can usually be hammered out fairly easily.

I do caution you, though, whatever you do, be sure to handle the bookings yourself. This is the best way to keep them honest. Here's the scenario . . . you advertise and take inquiries for your property. You speak with a renter, and they say, "I want to book it," you give them the number, and say, "Call this number tell them you want the Karpinski unit #1234." The renter calls that number, engages in conversation with the management company and just makes one comment about something that they were looking for . . . like, "Well, we really wanted a place with two fireplaces, but we spoke with Christine, and we have decided her place will be better." Now, the management company takes this opportunity and says, "Well, we have so-and-so unit down the road and that has two fireplaces . . ." Guess what, my friend? You just lost out on that valuable rental!

Finally, what should you do if you already have a management company, but now you've decided you want to get rid of them? When is the best time fire your management company? I do not recommend that you end a contract with your management company in the middle of peak rental season. I would be leery of that scenario because most of the vacationers have already booked their accommodations. Since most of the bookings are made 60 to 90 days before the peak season, I suggest that you get yourself through the peak season. Then, start advertising your property on the Internet in your off-season and transition into self-management for next year's peak rental season. Or, as an alternative, you may want to call your management company and talk to them about partnership programs.

By now, I think you get the point. Cut out the middleman and you win. Yes, there will be a little more work involved, but in the long run it will be well worth it. And as one season melts into the next, you will become more and more proficient at managing your own property. You may even want to give yourself the commission you save, and go take a vacation.

6

Effective Advertising

Advertising is powerful. Think about it. How else could you convince people that smoking is fun and that light beer really tastes good? Madison Avenue spends billions every year to get its messages across, and succeeds with often alarmingly effective results. Jack Simpson, a seasoned real estate columnist, once wrote, "Advertising is a powerful tool . . . without it, your business is dead. If you ever run out of money, cut your pay, cut your staff, quit paying your bills, but DON'T ever stop advertising. Because if you do, it's all over!"

Another wise businessman said, "Eighty percent of all advertising is wasted. The trick is to find out what draws the other 20% in."

Indeed, one of the keys to being successful in the vacation rental business is the effective use of advertising. Ideally, you want renters to look for you. You don't want to have to look for them. So, how exactly do you do that? Well, even in this Information Age, newspapers still have a role to play, but not the ones in major metropolitan areas. Advertising prices in metropolitan newspapers are outrageous! And, let's face it, very few people these days spend the time and effort to scour big city newspapers looking for vacation rentals. Your print advertising dollar would be better spent on an ad sheet in your office, in a church bulletin, or in a small community newspaper. These forms of advertising have proven to be quite effective and not too expensive. In fact, sometimes the local newspaper can be the *only* way to find certain rental properties. Last summer when we visited upstate New York, I couldn't find a single rental online. So what did I do? I dug out the local newspaper and started looking. Sure enough, we eventually found a place.

Still, in my experience, I have found that the Internet is the first place that a potential renter will look when researching vacation spots. These days, when people want to buy concert tickets, real estate, flowers, gifts, you name it, the Internet will have it. And, the good news is that websites can be 100% effective in renting vacation properties as long as they are utilized to their fullest. Plus, the cost is remarkably low.

It gets even better—you don't have to be a computer wiz. You only have to know how to email and surf the Web. Of course, if you don't own a computer, then it's nearly impossible to successfully rent by owner. But there really is no reason why you can't own a computer these days. The prices have dropped dramatically, and you can scoop up a decent desktop PC (including monitor) for $500 or less. The cost for a laptop is slightly more, but well worth it, since you can bring it along with you and keep track of things when visiting your vacation home or traveling on other business.

Internet Advertising

So now I've convinced you that the Internet is the way to go. Great, welcome aboard! But the World Wide Web is incredibly huge. How in the world are you going to get your message out there amongst all that clutter? Won't it get lost? No, it won't. That is, not if you do it the right way. New York City is a big, crowded place too, but with a good map or, even better, a competent tour guide, you can get exactly where you want to go. Let me be your Internet tour guide.

We're now at the point where you need to become familiar with four different kinds of websites. They are:

1. vacation property listing services (portal sites)
2   specialized websites
3. universal websites
4. personal websites

Let's examine each of them.

Vacation Property Listing Services (portal sites)

Vacation property listing services are websites that advertise vacation property for "rent by owners" (see Appendix 2 for a list of such websites). The main purpose of these sites is to put renters seeking accommodations in touch with vacation property owners. I call these types of sites "portal sites." Most portal sites charge a fee ranging from $50 to $150 per year (some are free), others charge on a three to six month basis, and a few charge by the number of hits or clicks. On portal sites, you can enter information about your property such as a description, the number of bedrooms, amenities, etc. You can even upload photos of your property. Some portal sites will allow you to add a link to a personal website (described later). The portal sites will then do all the necessary marketing (such as search engine ranking) to help renters find you and help you find renters.

What is important about portal sites is that they help the renters see, feel, touch, and imagine your property. It makes them want more. A portal site is basically a gateway. Think of it as the classified section of your newspaper. Let's say you are looking to buy a new Toyota. You pick up your local paper and turn to the automobile classified section. Now, why did you go to that section and not to the sports pages? Because you had a purpose in mind ... to find a car. It's the same with portal sites. They are like the classified section of the Internet. You bought the entire newspaper, but you were only interested in one specific section. It's the same with the Internet—all of it's available to you, but you're looking for something very specific. Yes, it is like finding a needle in a haystack, but with modern search engines, it is actually quite easy to find exactly what you are looking for. The portal sites will do search engine linking for you, so that's one less thing you have to worry about. When a person is looking for a vacation rental, in all likelihood they will end up at one of the major portal sites that are designed precisely for that purpose. There are hundreds, possibly thousands of such sites online.

That being said, all portal sites are not created equal. You as the owner want to make sure you use a portal site that is effective and easy to use. A portal site should be easy for you to use and more importantly, easy for the renter to use. Attributes that make a portal site effective and easy to use are:

For The Owner

Basic features that all portal web sites should have:

- The ability to easily create initial listing in a comprehensive manner, including detailed property descriptors, photos and pricing information.
- The ability to update and change your rates, photos and other listing information on a regular basis.
- Optimized search listings at popular search engines, meaning the site should be listed within the top 10 for search engines in your category. After all, this is how your renters will find you in the first place.

Advanced features that are nice to have but not always available:

+ Property availability calendars and reservation request forms.
+ Foreign language and currency conversion to expand potential renter audience.
+ Robust reservation management tools for inquiry management and reservation processing, including automatic rental contract generation and secure storage of renter contact information.
+ Simple tools to help with revenue tracking and year-end tax preparation.
+ Optional tools for reservation services, if you are busy and want to take advantage of a professional inquiry and reservation processing service.
+ Advertising means other than the internet. See if the web sites are advertising in magazines, newspapers, chambers of commerce or any other print advertising. This advertising should be targeted to the vacationers (not for them to bring in listings).

For the Renter

+ It provides multiple ways to find rentals by browsing listings or searching.
+ The ability to browse or sort listings by meaningful categories i.e., area, number of bedrooms, rates.
+ Search by available dates.
+ The ability to easily view availability through a calendar.
+ Telephone number for the portal site to assist renters or take complaints about properties.

Just as the classified section of the newspaper limits the size of your ad, portal websites generally have limited space or fields available for you to fully describe your property. In addition, some specialized websites will not allow you to link to a portal website page. So for this reason, I advocate that you also build a personal website.

Specialized Websites

In addition to portal sites, there are a number of specialized websites that you can utilize for advertising your property. These are websites that cater to the particular needs, desires, or interests of certain groups of people. Some of these sites are devoted to listing vacation properties and others are not. Some will have a designated area where you can add your property, but on others you may have to do a little digging to find an area for you to add your link (your personal website address).

The best example of a specialized site that is devoted to vacation property listings is www.petfriendlytravel.com. The main objective of the site is to connect a targeted group of renters (pet owners) with a specific group of property owners (those who accept pets). Most specialized sites work much like portals, allowing owners to enter property descriptions for a yearly fee.

But don't restrict yourself to specialized sites designed specifically for renters. A good example would be www.flyshop.com, which does not have travel as its primary purpose. It is *Fly Fisherman Magazine*'s website. The main purpose of this website is to sell the magazine. You'll find all sorts of information, of course, about fly-fishing. However, as you look more deeply into the website, you will see a section called "Travel Center." Go there and you can add your link to your cabin or home located in a fly-fishing area.

There is also a third type of specialized website that does a little of both, draws in the vacationers looking for accommodations, as well as people visiting the site for a special purpose. Examples of these would be chamber of commerce or local area websites. Let's look at a chamber of commerce site, for example. It will have all sorts of area information including shopping, restaurants, local festivals, activities, and accommodations in that particular area. So this website may draw people to it for many reasons, not just to look for accommodations. Most chambers' websites will also allow you a link to your personal website, most often for free to members. How do you become a member? Most only require you to be a sales tax collector, which most of you will be. So be sure to take advantage of this valuable perk that is available to you.

Universal Service Websites

Universal service websites offer a particular service related to vacation travel. Most often, these will be included on your personal website (some portal sites will also allow links to these).

Calendar websites: Although most portal websites have calendars, most of the specialized sites do not. For this reason, you will need an availability calendar to link to your personal website. Rentors.org and Rent1online.com both have universal vacation rental availability calendars that can be linked to your personal webpage.

Mapping websites: The most well known of mapping website is MapQuest (www.mapquest.com). Maps from MapQuest can be linked to your website for free. Adding a property location map is very helpful for the perspective renter. Many would like to know where your property is located and how to get there.

Note: To protect your property and your guest, do not put the map link to the exact street address. For instance if your property is located at 123 Sand Street, link to only to "Sand Street", or a nearby intersection, "Sand Street and Beach Road".

Payment options websites: If you accept electronic payments of any kind, then most often you will be able to provide a link to that site. PayPal (www.paypal.com) is a good example of a payment options site.

Personal Websites

A personal website is a site that you (or someone you hire) build and maintain. The main objective is to have a site where you can give detailed information about your property. You will link your personal website to many specialized sites (and some portal sites). But do *not* think that your personal website will be your main form of advertising. That's not the goal. Understand that your personal website is only a selling tool to help describe your particular property and your rules, policies, and rates. Its basic purpose is to WOW the potential renter with more details, photos, and in-depth information regarding your property's unique features. You don't need to spend time or money to understand how to draw vacationers to your particular site. In other words, don't try to figure out search engines. (That would be like to trying to deliver newspapers to each person you thought might be looking for your classified ad in the newspaper.) Search engine ranking is a complicated task best left to professionals, portal sites, and specialized sites.

Now, here's something to keep in mind. If you think of the portal site as your online *classified* section, then your personal website (to continue the automotive analogy from earlier) is more like the car dealership, where the customer can come in, see the product for him or herself, and begin making a decision. You should think of your personal website as a place where renters can find all of the information they need to know about your vacation property (including lots of specifics that the portal websites don't allow). Providing all of this detailed information is your personal website's major purpose. And it should be designed and presented in such a way that most of the questions a renter might ask are already answered. That way, when the renters decide to go ahead and contact you, the point of their phone call or email message will not be to ask a bunch of routine questions—it will be because they are seriously interested in renting your property and are probably, at that point, very close to making a booking.

When building a personal website you have two main choices:

1. You can use the website space you receive through your Internet Service Provider (ISP), such as America Online, MSN, Earthlink, etc.

2. Obtain your own domain name, and find a place to host your site.

While using space you already have (through your ISP account) seems attractive, there are many benefits to having your own domain. The pros and cons of each will be discussed below. First, let's explain what each is and how to use it.

Personal Space from Your ISP

When you sign up for Internet service, along with your email address and dial-up, cable modem, or DSL service, you typically are given a small amount of website space that you can use to host a personal site. Check with your ISP; you probably have free space available to you. To view a person's personal website hosted by an ISP, Internet users will have to enter a website address that follows a pattern similar to the following: home.emailaddress.earthlink.com.

Note: Sometimes you can purchase a domain name and redirect the address to your ISP. If you do so, be sure to cloak, or hide, the address forwarding so that your chosen domain name remains displayed.

Registering Your Own Domain Name

Your second choice, and the one I recommend for developing your personal website, is to register your own domain name or Internet address and an associated email address. For example www.howtorent byowner.com and christine@howtorentbyowner.com. Domains can be purchased for a year-long period with an annual renewal option. The cost to register a domain can vary significantly, however, most are $35 or less per year. I recommend www.godaddy.com, where registrations are $9 per year.

Once you have registered your domain name, you need to find a place to host your site. Hosting companies also vary greatly in price and in degree of service. I suggest you look for basic service only. After all, you only have one property to list, not a whole store full of products.

Why Choose a Domain Name Instead of ISP-Provided Web Space?

You may ask, why should I go to the trouble and cost of registering a domain when I may have personal web space already at my fingertips? A domain name is permanent (so long as you renew yearly). How many times have you changed Internet companies? Each time you do so, you have to notify all your friends that your email address has changed. Well, with ISP-provided web space, you'll have to move and/ or rebuild your website too. What a pain in the neck! This also means that anyone who has bookmarked your site will now have an address that no longer works. And, what about all of your previous renters? How will they contact you again?

So you see, building a personal website with your own domain name can help you build a brand name, or a name everyone will remember for your rental property. For example, HowToRentByOwner.com is much easier to remember and gives more of an air of professionalism than http:// home.christinekarpinski.aol.com (try saying that one three times fast).

Another major advantage of having your own domain name is for your property value. Yes! When you go to sell your property, think of the advantage of saying, property with a great rental history *and* complete website is included. Now you're selling an established business rather than just another property.

Building Your Personal Website

There are several ways to build your own website. You can hire an individual, (college students can typically do it for $100 or so), or you can hire a web design company (they can be very expensive). Or, you can do it yourself. "What?" you say, "I have no idea how to do it. I have trouble even programming the VCR! How am I ever going to design my own website?"

Relax; it really is easier than you think. If you can navigate your way through a program such as Microsoft Word, then you can build your own website. I did. You can even take a class through a learning center (see Appendix 6) or through the continuing education classes of most counties and universities.

I suggest you try one of the many online programs where you can purchase the domain name, as well as develop and maintain your website. These all-in-one sites are inexpensive (between $5–$10 per month). And, they tend to be very user friendly. One such site is www.godaddy.com.

Now, what should you call your website, and what should you use for an email address? Try to tie the name of your personal web-site to your vacation property so it's easy to remember. For example: HuntingCabin.com or FlyFishing.com. Then devise an email address that easily attaches to the website, such as hunt@huntingcabin.com or dan@flyfishing.com.

Which Are the Best Websites for Advertising Property?

People often ask me, "What is the best website to advertise on?" There's no good answer. Each property is unique and what will draw one type of vacationer will not interest the next group. You have to find websites that are directly related to your renters' needs and interests. Some of my clients do not use any of the bigger sites at all, and they are very success-ful. Take for instance, my Hot Springs, North Carolina, clients. They are not listed on any big portal websites. Hot Springs owners get all their bookings by advertising on a tiny site that only features Hot Springs properties, and websites specifically devoted to hiking the Appalachian Trail. The important thing is not the size of the websites. The impor-tant part is that the owners' and renters' specific needs are being met.

There are considerations only you can determine. Are you near a marina, skiing, scuba diving, or casinos? Do you accommodate pets, handicapped vacationers, or senior citizens? There are specialty sites for all these types of properties and more. Get the picture? So you have to think like the renter. Is he or she a skier, a scuba diver, a night-life devotee, or a big kid? Renters are going to decide based on their interests and their families' interests.

Decide what unique features your property has to offer and advertise accordingly. Imagine for a moment that you are not the owner. You are the renter looking for *your* property. Where would you begin? To find the best websites to advertise your property, you must think this way. Go to any search engine and type in what words you think the renter would search for to find your property. Look at the first few sites in the search results. Ask questions like, are there other properties on this site in the same area as my property? Contrary to popular belief, it's generally better to be listed on sites that have other properties in your area. Renters like to have choices, and if you are the only property listed in your area, chances are that the renters will move on to the next website that has more choices. Don't be shy either. Email the owners of a few properties and ask, "How well is this site working for you?" You may think of this as asking the competitors for advice, and it may seem odd, but this is a field where most people are not business people in the ordinary sense. Not in the cutthroat sense of big business where this may be considered privileged information. Many owners are happy to share their positive experiences.

It is important to list on multiple websites, at least three to five of them, for maximum exposure. It's still quite cost effective. Even listing on three sites will cost less than $500 per year. Rent your place for one week, and you've made your money back. How many sites you need to list with is a simple matter of supply and demand. If you're listing a property in a very popular destination, you might be able to get away with listing just one to three sites. However, if your vacation property is in a somewhat obscure area, it would probably be wise to list it on five websites. In some situations, cross advertising makes a good deal of sense. For example, in Colorado, I know that many vacationers check both the Internet and ski magazines. The owners, quite logically, advertise in both.

On Your Websites

On your websites, you will need to include some pertinent information about your property. The portal websites will vary a bit from one another. But most will have fields where they want you to enter relevant data about your property. If they do not have specific fields, be sure include all your information in your description. Here is the standard information you should provide:

One-Line Description

They usually first ask for a brief, one-line description of the property. Here's an example of a one-line description: "Immaculate 3 BR, 3 BA condo, ocean front, great for families." Notice that the abbreviations are the very same kind you would use in a newspaper classified ad. This will be the attention grabbing line that captures your renter's interest—the line that makes them click on your ad out of hundreds of choices.

More Detailed Description

Then you will need to write a second, more detailed description (however, even these will sometimes have a limitation on how many total characters you can use). My recommendation is that you write three to four clear, concise paragraphs. Don't write too much, however, because you might lose the readers' attention. This is where you will give full detailed information about your property. This is your sales pitch. Refer to the next chapter on how to write a good description.

Photos

You will want to post some really eye-catching photographs too. We all know that old cliché about a picture being worth a thousand words. Well, it's true! Read Chapter 8 to learn how to take good photographs, or consider hiring a professional photographer for the interior and exterior scenes.

Note: Remember, photos have copyrights. If you're using a photo you did not take yourself, be sure to get proper permission from the photographer and/or publication where you found the photo. If your photos have any recognizable faces, it's best to get written permission prior to publishing them on your web site.

Contact Phone Numbers

It is an absolute must that you include your phone number, both on the portal website and on your personal website. I know there are some of you who are a bit squeamish about your privacy and are uncomfortable with the idea of posting your phone number out there for the whole world to see. Well, just keep in mind that this is a business. Would you want to do business with a company that had no phone number? Probably not, so you have to provide a number where the renters can easily reach you.

In addition to the numbers themselves, be sure to include your time zone (for example, Eastern Standard Time, EST 81).   Remember, not everyone will be calling from the same time zone. This is important because when you put yourself in the renter's shoes, you have to realize that they may be working their way through dozens of listings. When they reach yours, it would be best if they call at the right time when you will be there to actually take the call. Otherwise you might miss out on impulse buyers. Consider cell phones too. But don't purchase a toll-free number for reservations (if you have them at work and want your renters to call you there, then toll-free numbers are fine). Otherwise, they look too much like business numbers and renters may not hesitate to call you at 3 A.M.!

Email Address

Be sure to post your email address. Most portal websites will have a field where you can enter it. Some portals may hide your address and require the renters to inquire through the portal. This is for your protection. It helps to keep the spam down.

Rates

Quote all rates—nightly, weekly and seasonal discounted rates. This information should go both on the portal site and on your personal website. Don't think you can leave the rates somewhat ambiguous, perhaps drawing in the curious with the intention of hooking them on your property before hitting them with the price. Give an example of a specific seasonal rate. A list format works best for rates because it's easiest to read. Use dashes to set off each item and asterisks for special notations. Ellipses are great to draw the eye across the page and prevent a cluttered look. Be very clear and detailed to make it easy to understand your rates. Read Chapter 9 for specific pricing information and examples.

Additional Charges and Restrictions

You should also quote any fees, taxes, or additional charges. It's always a good policy to be as up front and honest as possible. Some portal websites will have a field for these, others will not, so you will have to input the information manually. In either case, make sure that you include this information not only on your personal website but on the portal site as well. Additional charges may include pets, deposits, cleaning fees, and more.

Restrictions would be things that you do not allow. The "don't even call me if . . ." items. The most common restrictions are: no rentals to anyone under age 25, no pets, no smoking, and minimum length of stay.

Amenities for Your Property

Many websites have check boxes for things that you have on your property, and some require you to just type them in. Don't overlook anything here; many renters want the conveniences of home and more. This is where you spell out everything you have. These would be things like a pool, tennis courts, hot tub, full kitchen, etc. There may be specifics such as linens provided, coffee maker, toaster, etc. If you have it, list it.

Local Attractions

Don't forget local attractions. People want to know what there is to do in your area. For example, many people might consider the Myrtle Beach, South Carolina, area as strictly beach. Renters might not realize that there are several attractions that would appeal as much as the beach, such as a nearby battleship, an impressive aquarium, a golfer's haven, and many other not-so-well-known local attractions.

Calendar

It is very important to display an availability calendar and keep it up-to-date. Some renters only look at properties with this feature. Most portal websites have calendars available or allow links to universal calendars. They save both you and your renters a lot of time.

Calendars on the Web are a newer feature (within the last five years). Here's an astounding and true statistic: the calendar feature on one of my websites truly changed my rental life! I went from 1,400 "Sorry, I'm booked" responses a year to only 200!

Caution: Do not mark your calendars booked until after you receive the deposit.

Testimonials

Be sure to add some nice comments that you have received from past renters. But what if you just started and have none yet? Then omit this for now, and add this feature later. All it takes is a little patience and a nicely kept property, and the compliments are sure to follow.

CHAPTER

7

Writing a Good Description (Ad Copy)

By Amy Ashcroft Greener

Here are some helpful tips from Amy Ashcroft Greener for writing better descriptions of your property. Amy is a vacation property owner, but makes her living as a voice talent in the Midwest. Her work credits include several years as a copywriter, as well as radio and television news reporting. I think this will give you some excellent guidance on how to write descriptions of your property:

I'll be blunt. Either you're a good writer or you're not. Most people fall into the "not" group, and that's okay. You can always hire a professional to write great copy for your webpages. Trouble is, very few owners do, and it shows.

Bad spelling, typos, run-on sentences, and poor copy structure are commonplace in vacation property descriptions.

Truth be told, many owners are capable of writing good, basic copy. Your work may not have the flourishes and flow of an experienced copywriter, but you can do it. The process is not overly difficult, but it requires time, some extra effort, and thinking beyond your personal perspective.

Think of your webpage as a sales brochure. If you picked up some literature from a business, and it had less-than-professional photographs, copy, and layout, you'd think twice before spending your money there. Same thing goes for a vacation property, only more so. Remember, people don't know you—or your rental—from a hill of beans. Here are the elements of a great vacation property webpage:

- attractive in appearance
- clear, concise information
- an easy to read format
- top-notch photographs
- extra features that site visitors appreciate, i.e., availability calendar, location map, guestbook, local weather, and rental agreement
- rate information
- contact information

If you present your property to others using all the above elements, your site will standout among the crowd. Of course, this assumes you have a property that is well maintained, regularly improved, and is a desirable rental! A great webpage isn't going to fool anybody into renting a dilapidated shack.

The copy is the nuts and bolts of your sales presentation. Most owners labor over this, yet it doesn't have to be that way. Like any task, if you break it down into smaller chunks it's easier to accomplish and less daunting. Here are the steps and guidelines we'll use:

1. interview yourself

2. make a road map for the copy

3. first sentence: 17-word maximum

4. one paragraph, three sentences

5. use key words that sell

6. proofread before you post

Interview Yourself

All good copy begins with a few good questions. Even though an owner may think he knows everything possible about his rental, writers have a different perspective. A writer can be objective and separate the chaff from the wheat.

Here's a list of questions to get you started. Some of the questions are meant to be thought-provoking, not necessarily factual. These are designed to help you see beyond the "2 bed/2 bath/sleeps 4" line of thinking. Good copy is based on substance, but it also has feeling and imagery.

If you're not physically at the rental, use photographs to help jog your memory. Spread the pictures out on the table, grab a notepad, and jot down some quick answers. Remember, you're not trying to write copy here; just go with your first impressions to develop a basis for your property description.

+ What three words best describe your rental?

+ What are the three best features of your rental?

+ When you are inside the rental, how does it make you feel?

+ When you are standing outside your rental property, what is it like? Are there noticeable changes with each season?

+ Describe your location and view. What do you see and hear around you?

+ Describe your location in terms of distance to prime destinations near you. (For example: a two-minute walk to the ocean;

five miles from Disney World; or seven blocks from the Theater District.) Write down several answers if possible.

- What draws people to the area?
- Why would someone want to stay at your property?
- What advantages do you offer compared to similar properties?
- What types of renters would you expect your property to appeal to and why?
- Walk into each room of your rental. For each room, do the following:
  1. List three things or qualities about this room that you enjoy most.
  2. Describe the furnishings and decor; how do they make you feel?
- What improvements have I made to this property?

Make a Road Map

Remember learning how to write a letter in school? First there was the date, then the salutation, then the introduction, followed by the body and the closing. Well, you're going to do the same thing for your rental copy, by breaking it down into smaller segments. That gives you your writing a road map and makes the job much easier.

Here are the segments you'll want to include. Think of each one as a separate unit or paragraph. The introduction must come first, but all the other units can be ordered in whatever way works best for your property.

Introduction: Just a Taste

Start out strong and make people want to read more with short sentences and words that create images. Think of an introduction as a welcome mat that brings them inside.

Location: Specifics and Advantages

"Where are you located?" is a question owners hear over and over. Location is everything, so be specific, but also use key words like "convenient," "private," and "close to town" to convey the advantages your location provides.

Sleeping Accommodations

Tell people exactly what to expect so there are no surprises. If you have a multi-level condo, describe where the bedrooms are located, what size bed is in each room, and whether you provide additional blankets, pillows, sofa beds, air mattresses, etc. Rentals often accommodate groups of people, so renters appreciate knowing more details.

Features: Make a List

Big paragraphs that are loaded to the gills with features make for challenging reading. Frequently, people glance across large blocks of copy and may miss important items. Lists are much easier to read, have better retention rates, and are a snap to write.

Benefits: Sell Me on Your Rental

Features are important, but benefits are what the customer wants. Tell them *why* your property is ideal for them. Will a week at your rental be a perfect getaway for their family? Will honeymooners enjoy romantic views from the hot tub? Will sun-lovers thrill to being able to walk out of the condo right onto the beach? Put pictures in their heads, and they'll envision themselves at your vacation home.

Wrap It Up

Two or three sentences are all it takes to close your sales pitch. Very few rental owners do this on their pages, and it's an opportunity missed. Keep it simple and brief, but warm and inviting. Remember, you want people to see you as a friend and gracious rental property owner, not a corporate hotelier.

Shorter Sentences

If I remember one thing from my first news writing class in college, it was that a lead sentence for a news story should be no longer than 17 words. Honestly, I can't remember the research my professor quoted, but I do know that long-winded sentences don't work for readers. Shorter sentences get to the point, and they stand out. An occasional longer sentence is fine, just don't make it the rule.

Three Sentences per Paragraph

This is my personal formula for keeping paragraphs from becoming huge blocks of copy. People in a hurry often glance over the big paragraphs and may miss good information. To counter this, I recommend that you keep paragraphs to three sentences. Sometimes you may need to have a larger paragraph and that's fine. Just balance it by making the other paragraphs shorter in length.

Use Key Words that Sell

Mention the word "free," and everyone listens. Use that word on your webpage, and people won't miss it. (I use it in our low-season rate specials. Guests, who rent three nights in the dead of winter, get one night free. It works.) There are several other words that scientists have proven as good attention grabbers, including:

discover	easy	fast
love	money	safety
save	secret	yes
you		

Now, for my personal favorite vacation property descriptors:

activities	centrally located	classic
clean	convenient	cozy
easy access	easy to find	exceptional
extras	fun	inviting
peaceful	perfect	private
quiet	relaxing	retreat
romantic	rustic	secure/security
spacious	warm	well-appointed
well-equipped		

You'll notice that beautiful, nice, spectacular, and magnificent were not on my list. These words are so overused—especially in titles—that they just don't have impact. Use them sparingly.

Using key words will help people imagine themselves in your rental. If you sprinkle the words "peaceful," "escape," "romantic," "quiet," and "couples" into your copy, you'll immediately draw the attention of empty nesters or busy young couples.

Proofread Before You Post

Use a spell-checking program to look for spelling and typographical errors. After you're done, ask three people to look over your property description. Choose people with good communication and writing skills and who will give you an honest appraisal. Ask them to review your writing for sentence construction, grammar, content, and effectiveness (would they be enticed to rent your property based solely on what they've read?). Don't publish your copy until you have three sets of eyes look it over and receive positive feedback. By having others review your copy, you can feel confident that you've written an accurate property description with real selling power.

8

Picture Perfect Rental Photos

By Amy Ashcroft Greener

"One picture is worth 10,000 words."
— Chinese proverb.

Put yourself in the shoes of someone searching the Internet for the perfect vacation rental. Welcome to the world of comparison-shopping on the Internet. Today's search engines bring up countless vacation rental websites from around the world in seconds. And, as an owner, all you want is just a little piece of the action to fill your calendar.

If someone does make it to your webpage, consider yourself fortunate. But now that you've got their attention, are you going to disappoint or dazzle them? Are your photographs the kind that makes a viewer yearn to see more? Or, do your pictures look out-of-focus, appear too dark, have no focal point, or are plain as vanilla yogurt?

Even worse, you may be among the handful of owners who don't even put pictures on their website, figuring people will call anyway. Trust me—you're throwing away money every day that you don't have pictures posted. People planning their vacations are spending hundreds and thousands of dollars in some cases. Would you spend that kind of money sight unseen? There are many vacationers who won't even consider a rental without pictures and automatically move on to the next listing. You've worked too hard to find potential guests; don't lose them by not having photographs on your webpage.

Another waste of your advertising dollar—poor quality pictures. Shoddy photographs do two things: they make it difficult for the viewer to envision your property as it really is, and second, they shoot down your property's image. You can write wonderful copy to describe your rental, but the pictures can tell an altogether different story.

So no more excuses—it's time to step up and make those pictures shine. You don't have to have an expensive camera or take a photography course to produce pictures you'll be proud of. It's all about having a good basic digital camera and the desire to take the best pictures you can. Yes, it takes more time and effort, but that's what will make people bookmark your page and consider your rental for their vacation.

Gearing Up

Digital photography gives an owner the greatest flexibility and ease when it comes to uploading pictures to a website. Film cameras have their advantages, and higher quality 35mm cameras can't be beat when it comes to capturing images. But digital cameras are much easier to work with when you're transferring pictures to the Internet, so I recommend you borrow or purchase the very best quality digital camera you can afford. The higher the pixel count, the more lines of digital information will be in the picture taken. Another consideration: a glass lens will give you better quality pictures. When you are camera shopping, ask which models have glass lenses and which ones are plastic and factor that in to make your choice. Also look for cameras that are powered by rechargeable battery packs, rather than disposables. Digital cameras are known to consume battery power at a healthy clip, particularly with heavy flash use. A rechargeable battery pack is a huge money-saver in the long run.

If you're not comfortable choosing a digital camera on your own, I recommend you visit a local camera shop. These folks know their equipment and can guide you to the models and price range that are best for your needs. You'll also want to ask about any accessories you may need so you can download images to your computer. Digital cameras usually come with a software program so that you can edit your photographs once they've been downloaded.

Another source for photo editing software is a printer manufacturer like Hewlett-Packard. My printer is from the PhotoSmart series where you can plug the photo memory card right into the printer. It came with HP photo imaging software that I actually prefer over my Nikon camera's software. With this very easy-to-navigate program, I can manipulate the sharpness, color, and exposure as well as crop and rotate photos for the best results. That's important because sometimes you'll have a really nice shot, but the exposure was too bright or too dark. With photo editing software, you can quickly and easily improve your pictures. As a rule, I recommend that you enhance every picture you put on the Web.

Get Quality with Quantity

Even with the very best equipment, you can still take poor pictures. Don't be disheartened, though. You can develop a good eye and be a better photographer with some practice. Well actually, a lot of practice. The beauty of owning a digital camera is you can take picture after picture and not waste a dime. Sure the battery will need to be recharged after awhile, but you've got nothing to lose by taking loads of pictures. When I photograph a room, I take at least 20 pictures but usually more. Why? When I get home and download those images (mind you I live 500 miles from my rental), I've got at least two dozen choices to work with.

OK, so you're still wondering how could you possibly spend all that time on one room for just a single picture? Here are a few reasons why:

- The camera flash reflected in the window and made a huge white glare spot.
- You moved the camera oh-so-slightly while shooting, and the image is blurry.
- Someone left a plastic trash bag or stepladder in the background. (Don't laugh, both happened to me.)
- You thought you had everything in the picture, but did not.
- The time of day that you took the picture washed everything out.
- The shade on a lamp appears crooked.
- The picture just doesn't look right; it lacks a focal point.
- The room is too dark and photographed poorly.
- The picture was horizontal, and it would have been better vertical.
- The picture was vertical, and it would have been better horizontal.
- Yikes, you're in the photograph because you stood across from a mirror.

Every single one of those examples has happened to me at one time or another. That's why taking a couple dozen shots is to your advantage. Another benefit is that you will take more time to do the job right. After taking one shot three or four times, you'll eventually move to another spot and try something different. It forces you to look for new ways to approach the room and photograph it. Sometimes the picture you took just for the fun of it turns out to be the best of the bunch.

Where's the Ladder?

Next to my camera, this is the one item you can't be without when taking pictures. Every photography studio I've ever been in has a ladder and you should too. By bringing the vantage point up a foot or two (or three if you're feeling bold), you change the entire feeling of the picture. It adds an intimacy to the photograph, because you're letting the viewer see down into the room, rather than across it. Larger rooms or those with open floor plans are ideal for ladder shots. You'll be surprised at how much more you can see looking slightly down on the subject matter. But please *do not climb up on a ladder without someone standing next to you*. It's easy to lose your balance when looking through a viewfinder. Have someone on the ground by your side as you steady the camera for the shot.

If you don't have a ladder handy, a solid, sturdy chair will do. But again, it's important that you have a partner steady you and the chair when taking pictures. Another option is to use natural ladders such as stairways, balconies, even kitchen counters. I actually kneeled on our kitchen counter to shoot into our living area when I didn't have a step ladder available.

The Secret is Staging

Staging is referred to in the real estate industry as the artful presentation of a house to potential buyers. This is most often seen at an open house, where you'll find soft music in the background, candles lit, attractive place settings on the dining table, posh pillows scattered on the sofa, the fireplace ablaze, or the smell of apple-cinnamon simmering scents. The whole idea is to entice visitors with a feeling of comfort and warmth and present a home in its best possible light.

Though we can't enjoy the olfactory sensation of simmering scents or feel the heat generated by the fire, a photograph can convey whatever we want it to. That's where you have creative license to design a photograph that best represents your property. The best thing is that staging doesn't cost much. Let's go room by room and look at possible staging techniques.

The Bedroom

The focal point is usually the bed, so an attractive bedspread or quilt along with pillow shams is paramount. Make sure the bed is impeccably made—no wrinkles or bumps in the bedding. Toss a trio of pillows on the bed and you've got "instant posh," as I like to call it. Use a silk tree or plant nearby to bring the outdoors in. Sometimes you may need to pull it into the picture to just frame the edge of the photograph (one of my favorite tricks). You certainly wouldn't leave a silk tree right next to the bed, but in a photograph it appears perfectly fine. Try using a lower wattage bulb in the lamps; it's softer and more appealing. Take pictures with the lights on and then with them off. Also, take photos with the curtains or drapes open, as well as closed. Be aware that horizontal mini-blinds will sometimes make wild "zebra stripes" if they let too much bright light through. Place a nice book or two on the nightstand, as though someone's been enjoying a good read. Chenille throws can also look nice draped across the edge of the bed or footboard. Again, take pictures with and without the throw so you've got choices if it doesn't look right.

The Kitchen

Kitchen photographs tend to look the most cluttered of all pictures posted on webpages. Blenders, toasters, coffee makers, microwave ovens, paper towel holders, radios, canister sets, towels—you name it—give instant clutter to a picture. Sure, that's stuff people need when they're at your rental, but do you want it to give the impression of a cluttered kitchen?

First, clear off all counters except for the necessities—the microwave, the coffee maker, and maybe a utensil caddie. Everything else goes in the cabinets (at least for the time being). Actually, I keep our blender, crock-pot, and even the toaster in our lazy susan—kind of a makeshift appliance garage! This is especially helpful if you have a small kitchen, as many rental homes do.

Next, get rid of knick-knacks if you have them. You know, those cute craft-show doo-dads that hang on the wall under the wall cabinets. Another potential clutter source is the top of wall cabinets. For years, people have strung silk ivy and displayed dollar store baskets in this space. Less is more in this case, and if you don't have a good decorator's eye, it's best to clear off the cabinet tops.

If you have an island or eat-in kitchen counter, it's nice to show off that area with appropriate flourishes. A wooden bowl of plastic fruit can look like a still life in the center of the island, while three simple place settings at the counter can look inviting to guests. Keep towels, potholders and oven mitts tucked away for the photograph session. And no magnets or sticky notes on the refrigerator; it will look neat and clean with nothing at all.

And finally, avoid bright, overhead lighting to keep the picture more intimate. I like to use the vent hood light or light over the sink to bring illumination in small amounts into the picture. If you have recessed or track lighting, you'll be in great shape because these disperse small amounts of light without overpowering the photo.

The Family or Living Room

This is one area you can have a lot of fun with. First, it's usually a larger room and gives you more opportunities for different angles and shots. Second, you can set the tone with the decor. And third, you can play with accessories here more than with any other room. For example:

- Toss coordinating pillows on the easy chair or sofa.
- Drape a cotton or chenille throw over the edge of the sofa.
- If you have a fireplace, make a fire.
- Angle an area rug on the floor to make the area more intimate.
- If you allow candles in your unit, light an arrangement on the coffee table.
- Bring a silk tree into the picture to add vertical line and color to the picture.
- Use low-wattage bulbs for added intimacy.
- Put a wooden checkerboard on the coffee table to imply that a game is in progress.
- Do not turn the TV on (it rarely photographs well).
- Make sure the pillows are arranged nicely and the sofa cushions are smooth.
- Angle furniture so that it fits the picture, not the room (an industry trick by photographers who shoot editorial layouts for magazines).

The Bathroom

By far, the bathroom is the most difficult room to photograph due to its size. Whether it's long and narrow or just small and average, unless you have a master bath suite, you've got a challenge. First of all, ask yourself whether this room *needs* to be photographed. If your bathrooms are pretty basic, no one will find those photographs very interesting. On the other hand, if you have a beautiful step-in Jacuzzi tub with a view of the mountains, you've got a winner.

+ Be careful of cluttering up the bathroom. Too many candles, towels, dishes of potpourri, decorative glass bottles, and cherubs can ruin a good thing. Pull back and keep it simple. Two fluffy towels placed next to the tub, along with an attractive bottle or two of liquid soap or lotion give the impression of a high-end spa.

+ It's hard to take pictures around mirrors, so keep in mind where you are and where the camera is pointing. In some instances, you may have to step outside the bathroom and shoot the photograph from the doorway—it's worked for me.

+ Bathrooms are typically brighter; so don't worry about dimming the lights here.

+ Please don't take a picture where the toilet is front and center. It's just bad.

The Deck, Hot Tub, Porch, Etc.

Believe it or not, a bright sunny day isn't always the best for shooting outdoors. The sun washes out colors and casts strong shadows (especially on covered decks and porches) so ideally a day with some clouds to soften the light is better. Besides lighting issues, outdoor photography has a few additional concerns. First, the season and weather you're experiencing and second, the background. If you have a beautiful place on the beach, then by all means you want a sunny day with blue or green water and lots of colorful beach towels and umbrellas. If you shoot during the off-season (even if it is sunny), you won't get the same feel as the beach in full swing. I have one picture that I took during fall that shows the lake around the corner from our chalet. The colors are breathtaking and give the viewer a look at another season at our chalet. When taking photographs outdoors, you're at the mercy of Mother Nature and her schedule. So be prepared when the conditions are right to get out there and take a lot of pictures.

+ Be aware of the background. If there's something odd or not very attractive behind your subject, move and see if you can frame it differently.
+ No people in the hot tub or the swimming pool. Unless you're a model, it's just best to leave it to the imagination.
+ Stage the hot tub. Take two towels, two wine glasses on a tray with a bottle of wine and you've got an instantly romantic setting.
+ Turn on the tub. Put the jets on high for maximum effect. Another trick: stand on a small ladder and take the picture from an angle off to the side for a professional look.
+ If you have adirondack chairs or beach chairs, stage them with towels, beach balls, a glass of lemonade, a hardcover novel, or any other appropriate item.
+ Set the table. Use attractive place settings to envision al fresco dining on the deck, porch, or balcony
+ If you have a porch swing, you can stage it with a book and small pillow.

Shooting 101—Good Composition

As an amateur photographer, I've been fortunate to work around professionals all my life. Here are some of the things I've learned from them along the way:

Take Both Vertical and Horizontal Shots

Most of us are stuck on horizontal—meaning that's the way the camera is made to be held, so we shoot pictures that way. Well it's time to get comfortable with vertical. Watch a fashion photographer at work, and you'll see the camera being turned every which way. Trust your instincts and shoot a room or area the way you feel it should be shot—vertical or horizontal. Then after several snaps, turn your camera 90 degrees, and shoot an equal number the other way. You'll be surprised at the results; a vertical shot can make a room with a vaulted ceiling seem even more grand, while a horizontal picture can bring width to a small, narrow room.

Find a Focal Point

Just as each of us has our good and not-so-good features, so do rental properties. Walk around a room and decide what its best features are. It may have several, and if it does, you'll need to take more pictures. For example, if you have a beautiful stone fireplace, it only makes sense to make that a focal point in a picture. But what if you have a big entertainment center just across the room—out of sight of the fireplace shot? You can try to take a picture that would include both, but it may not be possible without a wide-angle lens. If you can't include both, move across the room to another angle and see if you can get another shot—equally good—that highlights the entertainment center. When you review your pictures, you can decide which one works best.

Go Off-Center

Nothing in nature is perfect; so don't try to be precise and centered with every photograph. Off-center is good—it looks more realistic and is more pleasing to the eye. How many times have you seen a picture of a bed in a bedroom shot straight over the middle of the bed? Is it original? Is it interesting? Now take that same bedroom photo and stand as far back as you can from the corner and shoot across it diagonally. Now it's more artistic and makes the room appear larger because you're showing other features of the room—not just a big old bed.

Rule of Thirds

Think of your viewfinder as a blank piece of paper. Now mentally draw a tic-tac-toe graphic on it—two lines vertical and two lines horizontal. This is how artists and photographers use the Rule of Thirds to find pleasing placements for their compositions. The idea is that you work within the areas where the lines intersect. Of course, any good artist or photographer will tell you that rules are made to be broken, so don't use this as a steadfast rule. It's just a guideline to help remind you to keep your subject's focal point in the best possible position. I like to start by using the Rule of Thirds when I begin to take pictures, then shift the camera slightly so the focal point is now off-center. Then, take another shot where it's even further off-center, almost to the left or right edge of the viewfinder. This technique is what I like to call covering the bases. When you review your photos later, you'll be glad you gave yourself the additional choices.

Lighting

Each hour of the day, the sun moves overhead and makes very perceptible changes in the way a room looks and feels. For example, our chalet's living and dining room areas appear cold in the morning when the sun is on the opposite side of the house. Later, the exact opposite happens: between 2 p.m. and 4 p.m., the sun is so bright and strong coming through the high windows that it washes out the colors of the room. The golden hour for taking pictures in that area is late afternoon, usually between 4 p.m. and 6 p.m. This is an important factor often overlooked by amateur photographers. Take your time and watch how the sun affects your subject, be it the exterior of the cabin, the hot tub on the deck or the master bedroom. Determine the best time of day to shoot, and you'll be rewarded with photographs that are eye candy to vacationers.

As far as artificial lighting is concerned, take pictures with both lights on and off. Sometimes the warm glow of a bedside lamp will make a better photograph. Other times, a light may cause glare or may be too bright. Again give yourself choices—take shots with both lights on and lights off. If you have recessed lighting in your property, it really looks good in photos. These focused areas of light from the ceiling add ambiance without washing a room out. Overhead lights, especially big kitchen fluorescents, are usually best left off. Fluorescent light bulbs cast a cool hue on a room and are rarely flattering. Small lighting sources, however, can be nice touches in a photo. Illuminate the area over the kitchen range, by turning on the range hood light. Or a single light over the sink can brighten up the area.

The Bottom Line

After all this you may say to yourself, "That's an awful lot of work just to get a few nice pictures of my rental." And you're absolutely right. But when you get compliments from people saying how much they liked your pictures or how nice your place looks—you'll be glad you took the extra time. Think of good pictures as an investment in your investment, corny as it may sound. The future of vacation property rentals is changing thanks to the World Wide Web. With better-than-average photographs, your property will present a polished, professional image and give people a reason to email or call about your rental. Set your rental apart with pictures that say, "I'm that perfect place you've been searching for!"

Note: Remember, photos have copyrights. If you're using a photo you did not take yourself, be sure to get proper permission from the photographer and/or publication where you found the photo. If your photos have any recognizable faces, it's best to get written permission prior to publishing them on your web site.

Pricing—Be Right on the Money

The subject of pricing *anything* can seem a bit subjective. After all, what is a fair price for an airline ticket? A new car? A steak dinner? A vacation home rental? The standard answer is, whatever price the rest of the market dictates. So when it comes to pricing your property, it is important to be right on the money. Literally! Price will directly affect the amount of response you get from your ads. To get just the right price, you will have to do research (I told you that work would be involved) on other properties in your area and find out what these other owners are charging. The best way to do this is (yet again) to think and act like a renter. Shop around for rates. Log on to the Internet and start searching. Make sure you are checking out similar properties. It's helpful to compare apples with apples not oranges. You can also check with management companies that rent properties in your area. Do whatever it takes to make an informed decision on what you should charge.

One mistake that many owners make is pricing their property much lower than their competition. I caution you that while it's certainly acceptable to charge a little less, maybe $10–$50 per week (to give you a competitive edge), pricing much lower may give the potential renter the wrong impression. They may think that your home is somehow inferior to the others. When I first started renting by owner, I was worried that I would have to give away the farm in order to get renters. I thought I would need to price my place significantly lower just to get the business. Fortunately, a phone call from a renter made me rethink this philosophy. He asked, "What's wrong with your place?" Shocked, I replied, "What's wrong? Why?" His response was, "Well, your place is so much cheaper, there must be something wrong with it!" That was a real eye opener for me. After that, I raised my price to be exactly the same as the other units in my building, and the rentals flowed in at a steady pace.

OK, let's look at the opposite end of this issue: what about charging more? After all, it may well be that your place has granite countertops, the most expensive furnishings, or other advantages that people may be willing to pay more for. And if you own a single family dwelling, you have much more flexibility with regard to rates because these homes can differ significantly from one another. So if your place is much nicer than the next guy's, you can indeed charge more. But, if you are a condominium owner, unless you own the penthouse, most likely your unit is laid out exactly like the rest of the units, and therefore, you have to charge the same. There's really no way around it. Yes, your expensive furnishings and fixtures can be used as a selling point. While it may be true that your place *is* nicer than the rest of them, in all likelihood this means that you will probably book faster and quite possibly more often than your competition. If you're going to charge significantly more than your competition, then your place needs to be significantly better.

Next, let's discuss the different pricing structures. By this I mean rates for specific seasons. Typically there are four to eight pricing seasons. There are the typical seasons—spring, summer, fall, and winter. But, you might also have other "hot" times within those seasons, such as spring break or fall foliage times, or maybe there's an event in the area that draws in many vacationers, like a festival or sporting event. These weeks you would probably want to price higher since demand is higher. But let me add a caution: don't make your prices too complicated.

Here's a typical listing of rates:

Season	Start	End	Per Night	Per Week	Per Month
Spring	Mar 01	May 25	$185	$925	N/A
Spring Break	Mar 23	Apr 20	N/A	$1,150	N/A
Summer	May 25	Aug 11	N/A	$1,350	N/A
Late Summer	Aug 11	Sep 08	$215	$1,075	N/A
Fall	Sep 08	Oct 31	$130	$800	$1,800
Winter	Nov 01	Mar 01	N/A	N/A	$1,100

Rates do not include 10% Sales Tax & Cleaning Fee. Pets OK with owner's permission ($25 fee nightly/ $150 weekly), $200 Security Deposit is required. Note: Until confirmed, rates are subject to change without notice.

As you can see from this example, the rates for each season have corresponding dates and prices for each time period. First, let's take a look at the corresponding dates. We all know that the seasons change in March, June, September, and December. But this owner's corresponding dates do not follow the calendar exactly. Did you notice that the summer rates start in May? This is because May is the highest demand. Your highest demand will be during the high or peak season. So if you have a ski place, the winter is peak season. If you have a beach place, it's the summer. You get the idea. This is the time when you can charge the most amount of money.

Looking more closely, you will notice that some time periods have nightly, weekly, and monthly rates, and some do not. This is for the same reason . . . it is based on demand. There is no need to quote rates for things that you wouldn't consider selling. This owner obviously will not rent on a nightly basis during the summer. Weekly rentals only. This is because the owner's quite sure that he or she will rent full weeks during this period. Why cut yourself short and allow someone to rent for three or four nights when you can have more income from the full week rental? And, on the same note, the owner does not show monthly rates either. That's not to say that he or she will not rent all four weeks of the month to one person, it's just that there is no discounted rate for that time period. After all, why give a discount on something that you can sell at full price? As always, it's all about thinking like a smart businessperson.

Let's look at the nightly rates. As you can see, they are not just the weekly rate divided by seven. There's a good reason for this. Nightly rates typically are $\frac{1}{5}$ to $\frac{1}{6}$ of the weekly rate. This owner can even advertise a special in the spring: "Rent 5 nights, get 2 nights free." Or how about this one: "Spring special: 33% off regular rates (summer rates)."

Now take a look at the owner's fall rates: $130 per night or $800 per week. "But," you say, "$130 multiplied by 7 nights equals $910." No need to get your calculator. Your math is correct. However, in this owner's area, the fall has a high demand for two- or three-night rentals, therefore, the owner can charge a higher nightly fee.

We also need to talk about monthly rates. Typically the monthly rates are quoted only during the slowest season. From this example, you can see the slowest seasons are fall and winter. Monthly rates are generally equivalent to a two- or three-week rental during that time period.

And be sure to clearly state all extra fees. Notice the footnote below the rates.

Rates do not include 10% Sales Tax & Cleaning Fee. Pets OK with owner's permission ($25 fee nightly/ $150 weekly), $200 Security Deposit is required. Note: Until confirmed, rates are subject to change without notice.

It's not a good idea to add the state sales tax figure to your price. The average consumer expects to pay sales tax. (Besides, the sales tax department likes to see taxes listed separately.) Also, let every renter know up front any other fees that will be assessed. And don't overlook the last line, about rates are subject to change. This is for your protection.

Pet Fees

For those of you who will accept pets (I think it's a good idea), it is absolutely appropriate to charge a daily pet fee. Think about it. Pet owners know and accept the fact that when they go away they have to pay for boarding for their pets. I, as an owner, do not want to *encourage* guests to bring their pets (pets can cause damage, but the risk is not as great as you imagine). If you do not charge extra for the pet, it could open up the door for this scenario . . . "We want to board Fido because he's such a pain. It would be nice to have a vacation without him, but it's way cheaper if we just take him with us."

Still, I would accept pets as a convenience for my guests. Just as the convenience items in the grocery store cost more per ounce, you too should charge more. My recommended pet fee is at least $20–$30 per day. I personally charge $25 per night and have never had anyone complain.

Minimum Stays

Many people ask me, should I require a minimum stay? As you can see from the example above, yes, it is advantageous to require minimum stays. The owner in the example requires a minimum stay of a week in the summer and a month in the winter. A lot of owners will not rent anything less than three nights, period. Others will do nightly rentals all year long. It's all a matter of preference and what your market dictates. The people who require three-night minimums mainly do this as a quality-of-life issue. It's a lot of work to coordinate daily check-ins and checkouts, not to mention the increased number of checks coming in as well as deposits returned for nightly rentals.

Discounts

Here's another one I hear a lot, "Will you give a discount?" Sometimes I will and other times I will not. It all depends on the situation. For peak weeks, I never give discounts. When there are times that are not easily rented, then sure, we can negotiate. Knock off 15%, the cleaning fee, or whatever you feel comfortable doing (but never knock off the sales tax). It's your place, and it's your call, but I will not give my place away. Remember, though, each time you allow a renter into your place you are taking a chance that things could happen. Some offers just are not worth it. Use discretion. You may get someone who wants to rent your place for 75% off. Think about it. Is it worth it? This is not some deep discount hotel. If you are doing everything right and renting all of your peak season and achieving positive cash flow, you shouldn't need to take that risk.

Be careful not to give discounts too early. I make a general rule that I will not give a discount until three weeks prior to the rental date. Learn from Duke's example:

Duke got a call from a renter 11 months prior to the rental date. They wanted to rent the last two weeks in April and asked if he could receive a discount if he rents for two weeks. Duke looked back at his past three years and had never rented those two weeks. So he agreed. He was generous and gave them 30% off his normal April price. Now the time passed and in January, Duke started getting a lot of calls for the week of April 19–26. He soon found out that this year Easter was very late, creating a high demand week that he easily could have rented for full price. Don't let this happen to you!

One final thought about discounts: if you accept credit cards, a common question from renters is, "Will you give a discount for cash payments?" The answer is yes. Just discount whatever percentage your credit card company charges you. Another caution: it's against the rules to charge an "up charge" for credit card transactions, so never incorporate that into your pricing. However, it is indeed acceptable to give cash discounts, so be sure to handle this issue appropriately.

Friend Rates

A question that never fails to come up at my seminars is: "My friends always ask if they can use my place. What, if anything, should I charge my friends?" Let me preface this discussion with this … the IRS looks closely at investment properties that are rented primarily for deeply discounted weeks. Does that mean you should not give discounts to your friends? No, the IRS mainly looks for investors who are using their properties mostly for their family and friends, but then use it as a tax shelter. This does not pertain to the average owner; we want to make money! So everyone knows you have a home in Hawaii, and now everyone's your best friend. Here is how I suggest you handle these folks. If your friend wants a peak week and wishes to book ahead of time, then by all means, let them. Just charge the full price. What? Won't they think I'm stingy, and not a true friend? Here's what I tell my friends. "This is an investment. And a business. If I give you a week for free, that's like taking $1,350 (the rental rate for the requested week) out of my pocket and handing it right to you.

If you would like a week for less (or free), then I will let you know when/if I have a last minute week open. If it's not booked, you are welcome to use it."

That may sound cold, but it's true. I am happy to let my friends use my place, but not if it takes money out of my hands. You may, of course, want to consider having a "friend rate." After all, they will be using the power, water, etc., and that will cost you money. A fair friend rate is between $25–$50 a night. And as a note of caution, I would not allow your friends to clean the place themselves before leaving (unless you require all renters to do so). This can be a friendship-breaker. It's best to have them pay the cleaning fee.

Donations, Trades, and Exchanges

Owning a vacation home can offer you some nice perks. You can exchange your place for other vacation homes, services, or even tax deductions. If you need maintenance, repairs, or work done, consider offering the contractor a week at your place instead of paying money. This can work well for many types of services that you need at either your vacation or personal home. Just be careful not to short-change yourself. Don't give away a $1,000 week in exchange for a service that you would only pay a couple hundred dollars for.

Note: Bartered services are taxable, so you must charge and pay sales tax on the bartered cash value.

Trades are fun and easy to do. One of the main sales pitches for timeshares is that you can trade your week and travel the world. Well, you can do this with your vacation investment property too. There are websites that charge a nominal fee for direct and indirect exchanges with owners throughout the world (see Appendix 4). You might also consider just contacting an owner directly from any of the various listing sites. It can't hurt to ask.

Donations are a nifty way to help out a good cause, and sometimes they can even be tax deductible* (check with your accountant). Think about donating a week that doesn't normally rent very well. Most charities would be happy to accept a week for an auction or raffle. Again, be sure to write in a clause that the winner must comply with all rental rules and policies. Be sure to also require a damage deposit.

By now you should have a solid understanding of the fundamentals of pricing. Become a market watcher and pay close attention to the rates of your competitors charge. Make sure that you know all that you need to about the significance of the changing seasons, upcoming holidays, and special events. Don't be afraid to be creative when it comes to bartering your vacation home for services or other useful purposes. And, by all means, never forget that this is a business. After you drum that concept into your head, the whole issue of pricing becomes so much clearer.

---

* Be sure to speak with your accountant or tax attorney regarding tax deductions. Blanket statements cannot be made concerning taxes. Depending on how the business is set up, how it's claimed on your taxes and the type and terms of the donation, your donation may or may not be deductible as advertising expense. This is a gray area, and you should have your tax professional make a determinaion on how it is applicable to your situation.

CHAPTER

10

Organizational Techniques

Organization is a difficult task for many people. With the fast pace of twenty-first century life, it is so easy to get snowed under an avalanche of paperwork. Computers are supposed to make everything much easier, but sometimes they only add to the confusion. Mass marketers recognize this modern dilemma. Why do you think there are so many ads in the newspapers on New Year's Day for organizational items? From Home Depot to Office Max, Wal-Mart to Walgreen's, everyone seems to be hawking all sorts of things that can organize your life.

Owning a vacation property and renting it out yourself can be very challenging to organize. You'll be taking multiple inquiries from different vacationers, often for the same week. This one's name is Mark

Daniels and that one's name is Daniel Marks, how will you keep track of who wanted which week? Or, how about this one: "Oh no! I booked the same week to two different people!" Then there's the paperwork involved, did you send out the rental rules for Mark or for Dan? Then the payments start coming in. Who paid? Who is due to pay? And who is due for a deposit refund? Then (yes, there's more) there's the property itself, did I service the air conditioner last time I was there or was it two-times ago? How about supplies? Was I out of dishwasher detergent or dish soap? Or was it trash bags I needed to buy?

Thankfully, I have some good news. There's no reason to get overwhelmed. Organizing your rental property business does *not* have to be a big headache. In fact, if you learn the right organizational techniques, it can run as smoothly as a well-oiled machine. But it is imperative that you get yourself organized right from day one. I want to share with you all the things that you need to consider. Exactly how you choose to do them is up to you. Just like some people prefer their pants be hung neatly in a closet and others choose to neatly fold them in a drawer. Neither way is right, and neither way is wrong, as long as the pants are not crumpled in a pile on the floor. The same is true for your vacation property. You can choose to use an organizer book, or you can choose to do everything on your computer. Whichever you are more comfortable doing is fine . . . so long as you decide on a certain system and stick with it religiously! Otherwise, it will not work at all.

For starters, set up your email program so that incoming rental emails go into a separate folder. Refer to the help section in your email program to set up "folders and rules." Be careful using any sort of email filters or spam blockers because most, if not all, of your rental inquiries will come from unknown email addresses. You may very well miss out on valuable rentals if you use these filters. Unfortunately, you will just have to deal with the spam (I know it's a pain in the neck, but just laugh at it, and delete it). This is precisely why you want a separate email folder. If you come in and have only two minutes to check your email, you can easily scan your folder to see if you have any new email inquiries. If you do, be sure to respond immediately.

Organizing on Your Computer

Welcome to the Information Age. A lot of organizational tasks can easily be done on your computer. If you are one of those people who does all their personal accounting on the computer, and you have a system that works well for you, then most likely you *can* do everything you need to do on your computer. If you are not currently 100% familiar with the programs associated with online accounting, however, now is *not* the time to learn.

I am one of those people who have been hesitant about computerizing all of my banking and business activities for my vacation rentals. Here's why. When are a lot of your rental calls going to come in? Not when you are sitting at your computer. More often, they'll come in the evening, when you're cooking dinner, or as Murphy's Law dictates, *while* you're eating dinner. When that phone rings and it's a renter, if you have to go into your office, wait until your computer boots up, and then open up the program where you have all your info, how much time will that take? I think it's easier to quickly flip the pages of a calendar and reply with a simple "Yes, I have it available," or "Sorry, that week is booked." By looking at your calendar you can figure out the answer in a matter of seconds. You could even respond when checking your voice mail from the road—just have that calendar with you, no computer required.

Now, here's something else you'll need to do to keep yourself well organized (I think you'll like this one) . . . keeping track of all the checks that come in. Yes, you can put them into Quicken or some other computer program, but you will have many checks coming in that should be deposited right way (you want checks to clear the bank *before* you send out directions). If you rent the 17 weeks necessary for the break-even cash flow formula, and use the deposit + 2 payments method, then the minimum number of checks you'll have coming in is 51. That's not 51 checks over 52 weeks; it's 51 checks over 12–16 weeks. Because of this, I prefer an organizer book.

If you are one of those people who would like to organize on your computer, listen to the opposing viewpoint of Bart Meltzer, vacation property owner and vacation rental software developer (www.rent1online.com) has to say about organizing on your computer:

"We own vacation properties in Hawaii that we rent by owner. We started of course with just one property. Back then we used the paper calendar method to organize our rentals. Then growing from a single unit to half a dozen properties, we found ourselves dealing with increasing inquiries, snowballing reservation information and a lot of paperwork, including inquiry information, reservation and accounting data, receipts, contracts, etc. Without a computer system, it became unwieldy.

Additionally, we like to spend time at our vacation home. So we needed to be able to bring our "business" with us when we traveled. We had to have a system that was mobile, accessible at all times, from anywhere, so that we would not miss out on valuable inquiries or reservations while we were away.

It is important to us that we organize our vacation rental by owner business like any real business. What we needed is a good set of tools to manage all aspects of the business from advertising to reporting at the years end. We found no suitable software available for vacation property owners. So being a web developer myself, I built rent1online.com. When selecting a management program, be sure to look for these key elements:

- Accurate Calendaring and Scheduling
- Reservation Data and Payment Data Management
- Month End Accounting
- Year End Reporting
- Web Based System

Calendaring

To avoid errors in double booking and other scheduling disasters, you'll need to organize a calendar of reservations. It's beneficial when these calendars can be accessible to a group of people from remote locations. This is especially helpfully if you are using a partnership program with a management company. You can also have your calendar available to your housekeepers and maintenance staff. One click of the click of the mouse should convert a reservation inquiry email into a reservation on the calendar.

Reservation Management

You must be able to track the life cycle of each reservation and all of the reservation details created along the way. Old reservations need to be archived, and inquiries that do not become reservations need to be deleted to clean up.

Accounting

You must be able to account for the income and expenses that make up the entire operation. Therefore, accounting organization is an important aspect of a home vacation rental business."

Organizing in a Book

I joke about it and call it my "Rental Bible." I do not leave home without it. Don't try to use a wall calendar, you will find those tiny little boxes run out of space too fast. Simply purchase an appointment book at your local office store, and customize it to fit your needs. Or, you can purchase the one specifically designed (by me) for vacation property rentals, *The Vacation Rental Organizer*.

If you purchase *The Vacation Rental Organizer*, all of the information is self-explanatory. Just fill in all the blanks and you are good-to-go. If you choose to make your own book, then be sure it has some pages for vital information pertaining to your property, such as lock box codes, financial information, and home owner's association information. You'll also want a few pages dedicated to contact information for maids, maintenance people, and networking (other owners' in your area). Don't forget to also have property inventory pages such as appliance makes, models, and serial numbers (in case you have to make a service call from home). And leave some pages for a ledger of income, expenses, and sales tax.

Determine how most of your booking will be reserved and set up your book accordingly—either nightly, weekly, or monthly. Next, you will need to decide whether to rent Friday to Friday, Saturday to Saturday, or Sunday to Sunday. The norm for rentals is generally from Saturday to Saturday. This works well for most renters because they can leave their homes on a day off from work and come home and have a day to unpack, unload, and unwind before starting the workweek. There are some owners who rent their property from Sunday to Sunday successfully. The advantage is that if you have a week open, you can easily rent the weekend (Friday and Saturday) and checkout Sunday, and still have a weekly renter follow, checking in on Sunday. Also, for destinations that most renters will fly to, sometimes it's less expensive and easier to get flights on Sundays. Fridays, on the other hand, tend to be a very busy and expensive travel days. The disadvantage to renting any period other than Saturday to Saturday is that people are creatures of habit. Most renters look for Saturday to Saturday, but you would rarely lose a rental over it.

In your organizer, you will want to keep track of all inquiries and bookings you get from renters. Develop a system (in your book) of jotting down notes about each person you speak with so that you can refer back to who they are when you have further conversations (either email or phone). Don't forget to keep track of where the renters found you. When it comes to portal renewal time (payment due to the listing sites), you will want to know how many qualified inquiries came from that site. By qualified, I mean how many inquiries actually resulted in a booking. Don't just count your emails. From one of my listing sites, I got 30–40 rental inquiries a week, but I never had one booking, so I did not renew my membership to that site. In other words, make sure you are getting enough bang for your buck.

Another thing you should make a habit of is photocopying each check you receive from renters. If you do not have a copier at home, most banks will photocopy them for free when you are depositing. Take that copy of the check and staple it right into your book. This will make it very easy to see if you have received a payment or not, as well as give you all the renter's information (name, address, etc.) from his or her check. Also, this is a good practice for income tax purposes. At year-end, or God forbid during an audit, you will have all the information available at your fingertips.

As for signed and returned rental rules and payment agreements, no need to staple these into your rental book. They will make your book too bulky. Just file them away. The only time you will need these is if you have problem renters, which (thankfully) is not often. If you do have a problem renter, and you have to keep a portion of the security deposit, then you'll want to staple that correspondence into the book.

You will also want to keep good track of the various services you pay for. Keeping up with the maid's payments, lawn maintenance, and other weekly or per-rental maintenance bills can easily get confusing (it's happened to me), especially if you are working with an individual who does not have a formal billing system established. Be sure to write in your book the check number that you paid with and it's corresponding billing date.

Another major advantage of keeping all this information in a book is when you go to sell your property, you can easily show the buyer the past records proving your rental history. Yes, you can print the documents off a computer program, but computer printouts are easily manipulated and sometimes are viewed as less credible.

In case I still haven't convinced you how important this rental book is, let me share a story with you. Perhaps my personal experience will get the point across. It happened a few years ago.

A week before one of my seminars, I got a call. My dear great aunt in Tampa had a stroke. I hopped on a plane to be there for her, and I took my rental book along (of course, I don't leave home without it). I had only expected to stay two days. While I was there, she passed away. Naturally, I stayed for the funeral. Now I had to fly from Tampa to Destin for my seminar. The problem was, all my seminar materials were at home.

> Thankfully, the flight from Tampa to Destin makes a stopover in Atlanta (my home town). So my husband agreed to meet me at the airport and give me all the necessary stuff for my seminar, but I had to have no carry on luggage. I was faced with a dilemma. No carry-on luggage would mean that I would have to check my luggage, and my rental book would have to go inside . . . out of my hands . . . and risk getting lost. I had no choice, so I did it.
>
> Now, for all the traveling I have done in my life, I have never lost luggage. Well, I am not sure what I ever did to offend Murphy, but his Law followed. You guessed it, my luggage got lost! I did not care about any item in my suitcase more than that rental book. A lost wallet would have been easier to live with. As it worked out, my luggage did end up back in my hands, but the mental anguish I went through was not fun. The moral of this story: don't let this book out of your hands!

By now, I think you can see the importance of organization. Your vacation rental business will never work if you have little scraps of paper with scribbling scrawled across them. No, that's for your kid's lemonade stand. This is serious business. You need a well thought out system that works for you. Life can be hectic enough, so when you're offered a chance to organize things (which leads to *simplifying* things), I have three little words of advice . . . go for it!

CHAPTER

11

Choosing Renters

Who should you target, who you don't want to stay, who are the ones you are inadvertently turning away . . .

Wouldn't it be great if everyone in the world were honest and trustworthy? If that were so, you'd never have to worry about renting out your vacation property. But, we live in the real world, and (though this may not sound very nice) there are going to be some people you simply don't want to rent to. Don't go on a guilt trip over it. It's your property, and you have the right to use discretion. For example, I have found it quite useful to require a minimum age. I will not rent to anyone under 25 or to college students. Ever been to a beachfront hotel during spring break? I once visited a hotel manager surveying the damage left in the wake of one of these raucous annual events. Broken and empty beer bottles in the elevators, mayhem in the rooms, half-finished fast food containers rotting on the beds, and more trash than I care to remember strewn all over the place. The manager shook his head, sighed, and said, "Hey, we're just happy to survive spring break."

Well, this ghastly scene does *not* have to happen to you. After all, you own the place, and it can only happen if you let it happen. An open door policy may sound fair, but this isn't about being fair. Like the manager said, it's about survival. And while this policy of no college kids has its obvious disadvantages (lost potential customers), it has some major advantages also. You are only a small businessperson and, unlike the George V Hotel in Paris, you can't afford to cover the repairs that a rock-and-roll band might do to the property. A bunch of college kids can sometimes trash a place even worse than Led Zeppelin in the group's heyday!

At this point, you may ask, but is it legal to have these kinds of restrictions? What about all of those fair housing laws the state and federal governments have enacted? Will I end up with some ACLU lawyer after me? Relax. Here is what the law says: "Title VIII of the Civil Rights Act of 1968 (Fair Housing Act), as amended, prohibits discrimination in the sale, rental, and financing of dwellings, and in other housing-related transactions, based on race, color, national origin, religion, sex, familial status (including children under the age of 18 living with parents of legal custodians, pregnant women, and people securing custody of children under the age of 18), and handicap (disability)." Did you notice that *age* is not written into the Fair Housing Act? Take full advantage of that. You are indeed allowed to have a policy stating age exclusion (i.e., no students, or no one under 25, only 55 years and older, etc.). Check with your local city and state for exclusions in your state to these laws regarding transient rentals.

Screening Your Guests

Properly screening your guests is your most important duty as an owner. You *must* screen each guest. *Never take a booking without speaking to your potential renter on the phone.* If you do not have time for this very important step, then maybe this is not the right thing for you. I'm dead serious about that. To omit this step in the process could be disastrous.

Often, you will have many email conversations with your potential renters, which may give you a certain amount of comfort. But you never know who is really behind that computer in cyberspace. You have invested too much time and money to give the keys to someone you don't know. You may say, "Well, I don't know them when I talk with them on the phone either." That's where you'd be wrong, because during your telephone conversation you will indeed get to know them.

The phone screening process does not have to be a dreaded chore. We're not planning a funeral. We're planning a vacation! That's fun. In fact, it's a very satisfying task, especially when you get all the nice compliments and thank you notes from your renters after they leave. The screening process is a skill most people already have ... even though they usually don't realize it. Simply be yourself. When I'm speaking with renters on the phone, I am friendly and personable. My main objective that I want to get across is that they are renting my second home. I make it a point to convey that I am not some big management company or businessperson. I am a real and genuine person, just like them.

When screening guests, it's important to use your instincts. When a renter calls, I never say I have anything available until after I have done a bit of screening. (Even if I have had previous email conversations with the renter and told them it was available. ... I could have booked it ten minutes ago.) If you keep your availability in question, you always have an "out" ("Sorry, I'm booked.") that you can use at any stage of the screening process. Disclosing your availability to the renter right from the start may back you into a corner. Instead, when they ask for a week, I say, "I think it's open, but I'm not sure, let me check." Then while I'm "checking" we engage in conversation, and I get to know them.

First thing I ask is, how many adults *and* how many children? I may even ask the ages of their children. I engage in conversation and get personal. A lot of times your renters will share all sorts of information about themselves, and you will find yourself doing the same. I also use this time to be sure that my property is truly the right place for them. I look at this as being a travel agent. I am trying to match the renters' needs with the property. If they want a place in the hustle and bustle of the town and my place is secluded, I advise them to continue searching. What, you say? Turn down a renter? Sure. Think about it. Do you want someone to stay at your place if they are not going to be happy there? Do you want them to curse you out when they pull up and find out it's not what they expected? Think about the ramifications. If they are not happy, are they going to take care of your place? Will they call and demand a refund? Or worse, sue you for false advertising? Best not to go there! Just be honest. I have tried to talk many people *out of* renting my place. Some choose to rent it anyway, but at least they know what they are getting into, and they will respect you (and your property) for it.

In my experience, families with small children make the best renters. Now, I realize that some of you may be thinking, wait a minute, rent to people with small kids? They can be worse than college kids! What if they scribble crayon on the walls or spill grape juice on the rugs? In reality, this rarely happens. The risks are not as high as you might think. Also, in addition to cutting yourself off from at least 50% of your prospective renters, you may be violating the law. As I said earlier, you are allowed age restrictions, *but* you cannot discriminate against families with children under 18, unless your property is located in a place, such as a 55 and older community, that has obtained the licensing exclusions to do so. Even if you are still certain that you don't want kids, if I were you, I would not say so in my advertising.

Now, back to the conversation with my renters. Remember the first question: How many adults and how many children? If I hear "all adults," then my antenna goes up, and I adopt a different mindset, or I use my "out" . . . "Sorry I'm booked." (Just as in any game, it's best to hold onto your out until the very end, only use it as your last resort.) You don't want to rule out *all* people with no children, you only want to rule out those under 25.

So, your next question is, how will I know if they are under 25? Again, the answer is the obvious one . . . just ask. Believe it or not, most will answer honestly. If they answer honestly and are under 25, this is a good time to use your out. If they are truly over 25, then most often they'll be flattered and tell you all about themselves, making it that much easier to engage in conversation and get to know them.

Well, what if I ask and they lie? Sure, there are things that you could require as proof such as a copy of his or her driver's license. But really? Come on. If they lie to your face (over the phone) then chances are they'll lie to you in writing too. Kids have fake IDs. This would only provide a false sense of security on your part. How would you verify that the IDs they send are really their own?

Instead, when you are speaking with them if you feel that their voices or demeanors are that of people under 25, you can use your "out" right at this point. Or consider another tactic . . . how about something like this: "Well, I just have to ask and make sure that you are really over 25. Because, you see, I am not allowed to rent to anyone under 25. It's not my rule; it's the association's rule. Our home is in an association, and our by-laws state that we are not allowed to rent to anyone under 25. They're pretty strict about it too. If the association finds out, they will evict you, and I have absolutely no say in the matter. And, if you are evicted, then you lose all your rent and your deposit. I feel pretty bad for people under 25 years old these days. I was there once myself. I was very responsible. But it's always those few bad apples that spoil it for the rest of us." That usually scares them off, and if it doesn't I can always use my last out!

Sometimes you can get a lot of the preliminary screening work completed before even speaking to a potential renter on the phone. When you receive email inquiries, you can do a little detective work. Look for clues. Take a look at the email address. If it's something like big-bad-boy@college.edu, what's your first clue? Is it the Big Bad Boy? Possibly. But even the college.edu can be a clue. I would still reply to this email as I would every other. It could very well be a professor or an employee of the university, or perhaps a young person doing the search for his or her parents. You would not want to discount any renter just because of his or her email address; however, have your antenna up for screening.

Increase the Number of Renters

It's the one question people always want to answer: how can you attract more renters to your property? The first thing you must realize is, the more restrictive you are, the fewer renters you will have. While it's certainly acceptable to have any policies and restrictions that you want (inside the law), you must also acknowledge that the more restrictions you have, the fewer rentals you will book. For some people, that's fine. But if your goal is to have maximum occupancy, then read on. You're going to learn the importance of flexibility.

For example, you may want to consider an exception to the under 25 rule. Ski areas are one place where many owners have a hard time *not* renting to people under 25, since many skiers are college students. If you think that this can increase your rentals, remember, there are plenty of responsible college kids . . . not all are bad! Take a large deposit, require a midweek cleaning at an extra charge (the maid can asses the property while she's there), and make it clear that you will not tolerate any "hell-raising." Tell them if you get a call from neighbors or from the police, then they will forfeit the deposit (write this specifically into the rules).

For those of you who wish to broaden your horizons a bit more, you might consider accepting situations that you previously ruled out. Remember, for every group of people that you exclude, you are writing off the possibility of renting to what may be a large pool of potentially good guests. This could very well include pet owners. I would venture to guess that over 30% of American households have dogs. Let's face it; there are some owners who won't leave home without their dogs. Therefore, they only look for vacation homes that will allow them to take Fido along for the trip. And here's a little secret: if people have a dog that they want to take with them, chances are excellent that it is *not* the kind of dog that causes a lot of problems . . . otherwise, in all likelihood, they would have chosen to leave him at home! It's safe to assume that they want a relaxing vacation, so the folks who want to take the dog along usually have a pet that is well behaved.

This can increase your occupancy and your revenue. When you accept pets, it's OK to take an additional $20–$25/night or $140–$175/week. That's enough money to get the carpet cleaned each time, or rent 8–10 weeks, and you have enough money to replace the carpeting! Pet owners expect to pay this extra amount, and it's in lieu of the boarding costs they would have to pay otherwise. The bottom line is that you will make more money. You will also take an additional deposit amount for the pet, so if the pet damages anything, you will be covered. And here's the icing on the cake. Vacation properties that accept pets increase their occupancy by 10%–50%! It's also a great way to increase off-season rentals. Let me tell you what happened to me. I always booked up for spring and summer, but rarely had fall bookings (my property has three bedrooms, and after the kids are in school, couples without kids are my main renters. These couples are only looking for one-bedroom places). So I decided to accept pets in the fall only, and I went from 1–2 weeks booked in the fall to having all of September and October booked! Needless to say, I've kept that new policy in place ever since.

A good example of changing your rental policies in a positive way comes from an owner I spoke with named Jennifer, who owned a nice cabin in the mountains of Colorado. She was within driving distance to three ski resorts, but not really close enough to any of them to advertise that her place was associated with any of them. She was only booking her cabin two to three weeks per year. She occasionally had a weekend booked off-season. I advised her to start accepting pets. The minute she did, her bookings started flowing in. Two years later, she is booked for the whole ski season, three or four weeks during the summer to hikers, and she rents 10–12 long weekends through the year. She has never been happier! She said that she has to clean the carpet more often but it has been well worth it . . . and she has now bought the cabin right next door too.

Sometimes it's not your policies that detract renters, but your property itself. There are, however, many ways that you can add things to your property (some less expensive than others) that will increase occupancy. Remember the group represents the largest percentage of renters—families with children. Think of things that will make families want to stay at your place rather than the next. I cannot tell you how many times people have called me and said my unit was not exactly what they were looking for, but because I have a high chair and porta-crib, they want to stay at my property. Those two thing things only cost about $150, and I have made my money back a hundred times over. Then there are things like toys, games (even video games), bikes . . . really this list is endless.

As always, a little comparison-shopping can be helpful. Look at properties in the area. What do they have that you do not? I know if you are in Colorado, don't even consider renting a place without a hot tub. In Minnesota, a sauna is a must. You may be thinking that these are rather pricey additions, but usually with the number of extra bookings, the additions will pay for themselves.

Another thing that people seem to overlook is the number of people you sleep. Now, I am not a person who likes to pack them in. I do not have barracks, but something as easy as a pull out sofa bed or a futon can allow two more people a place to sleep at night. This can very well be the difference between renting or not.

You may also consider making your unit handicap accessible. This can bring in more renters at no additional risk. You need to realize that handicapped people (not just older people) have a very hard time finding vacation properties to rent. Often they have to stay in hotels simply because they have no other choices. If you can buy a handicapped accessible unit, then go ahead and do so. If you already own, then consider updating your place and making it handicap accessible. I think you might be surprised to find that sometimes it costs very little to upgrade. Be sure, however, to refer to government guidelines when updating your property for handicap accessibility or advertising it as such. Note that there are different types of special needs accessibility: for example, wheelchair accessible requires a bedroom with 36" doorways and a roll-in shower. The bathroom, kitchen, and bedroom must have enough floor clearance for a wheelchair to turn 360 degrees. Another category might require 36" doors, bars in the bathroom, an elevator, etc. So be sure to carefully check out these requirements beforehand.

Let me say, however, that finding good renters is not as hard as you may think. You will likely get lots of inquiries. And when they call, there's no need for a hard sell from you (after all, they called you . . . not the other way around!). If there is something that comes up in the conversation that seems like a drawback to the potential renter (i.e., they were hoping for a great view of the beach, and your place does not have that) there are ways that you can turn that to your advantage. Listen to Cody's story:

Cody owns a home near the beach. You can see the water just a bit from her home, but nothing that could really be called a view. Every time someone calls his or her first question is, "What kind of view do you have?" Cody used to say, "Sorry, I have no view." The renters would say, "That's too bad. I'm really looking for a view," and that was the end of the conversation. Cody got pretty tired of having all those renters slip right out of her hand simply because she had no view. She had two options: the first was to sell her place and buy another. This was not a good option. Places with a view were $100,000 more, she couldn't afford it.

The second option made a lot more sense. She could change her tactics. And that is precisely what she did. Cody diligently searched the Internet for all properties that were on the ocean, with a good view. She found out that they not only cost more to buy, but they also cost more to rent. She realized she had an opportunity here, and she seized it. This is how she has changed her way of answering that same question—and how she now gets bookings.

Renter: "Do you have a view?"

Cody: "Sorry, when we bought the place, I really wanted that view too, but we just couldn't afford it. Then I started thinking, how much time am I really going to spend in the place anyway? I'm really going to be on the beach every day. So we bought this place. I love it. My place is great."

Renter: "Sorry, I really wanted the view."

Cody: "That's OK, I understand. Let me see, I do know of some other owners who have properties with a great view ... let's see, OK, here's the same type of unit as mine, two bedroom, two bath, great view. Do you want their name and number?"

Renter: "Sure, please!"

Cody: "OK, it's #24AB5 on website.com, John Smith #234-123-4567 ... wow, his place is really nice, nice price too."

Renter: "Really? How much?"

Cody: "Well, it looks like it's $800 more per week than mine, but it's nice."

Renter: "Oh, I really can't afford that . . . can you tell me a little more about your place, maybe it wouldn't be so bad not to have the view."

Cody is not selling the renter something they don't want; remember what I said earlier, the renter contacted her first. At first, renters want everything . . . the view, the large size, the location, the most for their money, etc. Then, when they narrow it down, they come to realize that they have to make compromises . . . and the only selling that you need to do is to help them with those compromises.

Another group of vacationers you may not want to rule out entirely are last-minute renters. Though your goal certainly should be to avoid such bookings (they just make life too complicated, and it's much better to have all of your rentals booked well in advance) sometimes things will not work out in this idealistic manner. That is when it is time to consider an exception to the rule. Many of the websites you advertise on will have bulletin boards where you can post last-minute specials. I think a better strategy is to change the quick description line you have created, the one that pops up every time renters search for vacation rentals using the portal sites (which bring them to a listing of properties in your area, including yours). Change your original description, for example, "Great 3 BR condo on the beach" to something like, "3 BR on beach, last-minute cancellation OPEN 11/19–11/30." There's an excellent chance that this one little change will make the phone ring.

So, you see, finding ideal renters involves much more than simply screening out a few bad apples. You need to be creative and give some thought to all of those people who might make great renters, if gave them a chance. Yes, by all means, exercise discretion, and don't just rent out your place to every person who comes your way. But don't be close-minded either. Become savvy with your "people detector" skills, and learn to identify people you think you can trust . . . and those you can't. Make exceptions to your general rules whenever you deem it wise. Let me finish with a story that drives home this point perfectly:

> The first year I owned my property in Destin, Florida, I was nervous about whether I would get renters. One of the first calls I got was from a mother looking for a place where her teenage daughter and four of her friends could go on a senior trip. "Mom coming too?" I asked. "Nope." Of course, my initial reaction was "No way." Then I talked with the mom, explaining my policies. She pretty much begged me and offered a huge deposit and reassured me that these girls were very well behaved young adults. They don't drink, smoke, etc. This mother seemed so genuine. And I am a sucker for a good story. I let the girls rent my place, and everything went well. I had no regrets.

> But the story didn't end there. Six years later, I got a phone call from this same mom. She said, "Christine, do you remember me?" "Of course," I said, "Your daughter and her friends were some of my first renters." She explained that her daughter had now graduated from college and was getting married (she was still under 25), and she loved our place so much that she wanted to spend her honeymoon there. Naturally, I gladly said, "Yes." I can't tell you how good that made me feel about my gut instinct decision six years earlier. So sometimes it is indeed OK to use your heart when screening potential guests. And who knows, you may just be securing potential renters for years to come.

CHAPTER

12

Taking Reservations

Before you accept reservations from renters, first you must understand the amount of time and frustration that renters go through in order to find you. So, I am going to give you an assignment that you must do before we move on. I want you to time yourself to see how long this process takes. (Pretend you're in school . . . "There's going to be a quiz on this later, so pay attention.")

First, look at the clock and make a note of what time it is. Then, think of a location where you would like to spend your vacation. Let's say Colorado (you can pick anywhere). Now figure out where in Colorado you wish to go. We'll pick Breckenridge. Next, think of the budget you want to spend, for example, $1,000 for a week. Then choose the dates you will want to arrive and depart. And don't forget that you have to find a property that suits your size and particular needs, say, two bedrooms within walking distance to the ski trails.

After you've made these initial decisions, go to the Internet, and start searching for three comparable properties that fit those criteria. Visit a variety of websites. Do whatever it takes to find them. Once you find three properties, look at the clock again. How long did that take? Can you find those three properties again? Did you bookmark them or write them down?

Most likely it will have taken an hour, two hours, or maybe even more. Since you did not follow through and actually contact the owners, you don't even know if the properties you picked are actually available. Maybe the owner didn't update his or her calendar, or the property may have been booked earlier today. What if none of them are available? Then, you have to start over again.

The point of this exercise is to let you experience what inquiring renters have to go through in order to find *your* property. I want you to realize that once the renter finally finds a property that he or she sends an email about, he or she is already at the point of frustration. They are eager to finally secure a booking. And if that renter hears back from all the owners saying they are booked, the frustration grows. They will have to go through the searching process all over again and will be even more eager to book the first place that is available.

View this as if you were buying any other product, a Honda Civic for example. Now, if you are buying a new Civic, you have plenty of options; after all, there are many dealers that have hundreds of them lined up in their lots. Well, let's say you don't want a new Civic, you want a used one. That's going to be slightly more difficult. If you are looking for one particular color or year, you may scour through the paper each week and visit many dealers. Once you finally find that one perfect car that suits your needs, are you going to think about it for a long time? Probably not. Most people would buy it right away. The same is true with vacation property rentals. If the renter wanted a hotel room, then he or she would have thousands to choose from. But a two-bedroom, two-bath place in Breckenridge might be a bit more difficult to come by. When they finally do find exactly what they are looking for, they will want to reserve it right away.

By all means, when they contact you, don't blow a potential rental by not calling back in a timely manner! It doesn't matter what your circumstances are or what is going on in your life. Make this a priority. Even if you (the owner) plan on being away, especially during the busy booking times, be sure to have someone you can trust check your email and/or phone messages so you don't lose out on valuable bookings. Let the following story serve as an example:

Shirley and her husband own a vacation property in northern Minnesota. Shirley handles all the booking when they rent it out. In August, she delivered their new baby boy. The last thing on her mind when she first got home was her rental property. After about a week, she finally logged on to her computer and found about 25 rental inquiries for fall weekends. Now, since all these inquiries were a week old, she decided instead of emailing back, she would call. She was amazed to find out that every one of these people had already found and booked another place. The renters were not just browsing, or whimsically searching, they were actually looking to book. She would not have traded her new baby for any amount of bookings but now, if she's going to be away from her computer, she has her husband or a family member check her email.

The bottom line is this: when you get an inquiry, either by phone or email, please understand and respect the fact that your renter has worked very hard to find you. Contact them right away! Even if you have it booked. More often than not, the first owner who picks up the phone and quickly returns the renter's call, or dashes off an email response, will be the owner who gets the booking. (Tip: When emailing a response, be sure to write something in your subject line so that the renter does not mistake your email for junk mail.) There are thousands of salespeople who would kill for the direct target marketing capability that we are so fortunate to have in the vacation rental business. Take full advantage of the marvelous opportunity opened up for you by modern technology. The Internet will make that phone ring. But it can't do the follow-up (returning calls and emails promptly, being well organized and professional, etc.). These important tasks are up to you. The key to being well organized is to write down the information for all inquiries and bookings in your rental book.

Telephone Communications

I never book a rental without speaking to the renter on the phone. Via email you never really know who is on the other side of the computer screen. Even if I have had numerous email conversations, I always require the renter to call me (or I call them). This gives me one last chance to screen the guest a little more closely (it's always better to be safe than sorry).

Don't take the phone for granted. It's a simple to use tool, but you still need a well-organized system. By doing business on the Internet, you have to remember that you will get calls from all over the country, maybe even outside the country. Therefore, you need to know the various time zones, and which state belongs with what area code. You'll need an up-to-date list because area codes change a lot these days. So if you live on the East coast don't hurry to return a call to the 310 area code at 9 A.M. That's California, and it will only be 6 A.M.! Here is a good area code website: www.bennetyee.org/ucsd-pages/area.html

There is no need to install a separate phone line in your home for taking reservations. This is not like owning traditional investment property where you don't want your renters to have your home number, know where you live, etc. This is quite the opposite. You want the renter to know that this is your second home, and that you are just a regular person, not some big company. You want them to feel privileged to stay in your home.

For this same reason, I don't suggest posting toll-free numbers, nor do you need a separate phone line for your renters to call you with questions, problems, etc. There are a couple of reasons. First the cost, and second, when they know it is your home they are calling and not some management company, they are less inclined to call you all hours of the day and night.

When it comes to telephone answering, I find it advantageous to have an answering machine with separate mailboxes, the kind you buy from your local phone company. The ones that say, "If you're calling for Mr. or Mrs. Paradise, press 1. If you're calling Judy, press 2. Etc." I suggest using this system for your rentals. You can say, "Thanks for calling. If you're calling about the rental in Destin, Florida, please press 1." When they get to voice mailbox 1, your message should assure them that you will call right back. And then really do it! This way you won't lose any bookings.

You can also use your separate mailbox to say something like, "I'm sorry, I'm totally booked until August 21. If you're looking for a rental after that time, please leave your name, number, and the dates you are inquiring about, and I will get back to you."

Here's a helpful tip. When you get into renting, you will begin to realize that there are patterns in certain days and times of the year that see more inquiries than others. You'll notice that on the first really nice sunny day in the winter, you will receive a lot of calls. Right after the first snow there typically is a spike in calls from renters who want to go skiing. Another very busy time is the week right before Christmas (This makes me crazy. I'm not even ready for the holidays and already people are planning their summer vacations!). Right after the New Year and around tax refund times, you will also see an influx of rental calls and inquiries. Be sure to check your voice and emails even more frequently during these critical time periods.

Put It in Writing

OK, so let's say you have done everything up to this point. The renter contacted you. You have spoken with them. You screened them, agreed on dates, and the renter wants to book it. Now what?

As a way to protect both you and your renter, you will want to put everything down in writing. You will want to send them a copy of your rental rules and billing confirmation (see Appendix 1). These documents are critical. You do not need to mail them; it's perfectly acceptable to email these documents to the renter. But do not send them as email attachments. Instead, copy and paste your documents into a standard email message as a regular text document (since many people do not have compatible programs on their computers—you may have Microsoft Word, and they may have WordPerfect). Have your renter print and sign these documents and send them back with their deposit check. DO NOT ACCEPT DEPOSITS WITHOUT SIGNED COPIES OF THESE DOCUMENTS. You may want to write something like this:

> Enclosed is our rental contract and rules. Please print, read, sign, and send it along with your deposit to the address below. Thanks so much, and if you have any questions, feel free to contact me.
>   Thanks again, Christine

Now we're ready to get to the good part . . . collecting the money.

Payments

When you think about it, this should be a rather pleasant topic, because what we're talking about is making money. People paying you to rent your vacation property. Sounds simple, right? Well, yes and no. Getting paid doesn't have to be difficult; you just have to put some sensible policies in place right from the beginning. There are, of course, a number of ways you can accept payment. But not all of them are created equal. The ideal form of payment, in my opinion, is personal check. What if the check bounces? I don't think there is much to worry about. I've only had one check bounce in all the time I have been renting. And that was an error. The lady used the wrong account so she apologized and shipped a new check to me overnight. Also, you will want to make sure their check clears well in advance of when they rent, so you are at not at risk of rendering any services before being paid (more on that in a moment when we discuss scheduling).

But wait a minute, you say, there are lots of people who will want to use other payment methods. OK, let's take a look at each of them.

Money Orders (or Cashiers' Checks)

Money orders and cashiers' checks are certainly an acceptable form of payment, but it has the drawback of not being very convenient. The renter has to go to a bank or post office and buy the money order (after withdrawing the cash to purchase it), before he or she can send it to me. That delay in the process is something I want to avoid (who knows, maybe he or she will change his or her mind between speaking with me and going to the bank!).

There is one important exception to my reluctance to accept money orders or cashier's checks—international guests. These people (in my case, many of them are Canadian) are, of course, using a different currency than you. In these cases, you want to make sure you get paid secured funds in U.S. dollars (or whatever currency you accept). The best way to do this is by asking for a cashier's check or money order. Since they are well aware that there is a currency difference, these guests expect a little extra inconvenience and usually have a very easygoing, accepting attitude about it.

PayPal

Originally started to accommodate the eBay and other online auctions craze, PayPal (www.paypal.com) is a payment method many people like because of its convenience. Essentially, a person can send you your money via the Internet. The money comes straight out of their credit card or personal checking account. Of course, you have to open up your own PayPal account to receive the money. But the process is relatively simple (compared to setting up a credit card merchant account), and the costs are small.

Credit Cards

We've all become accustomed to using credit cards for just about everything these days, from booking hotel rooms to renting cars to buying things in stores. For many renters, the deciding factor of which property to rent might just come down to the one that accepts credit cards.

First, if you're reluctant to take credit cards under any circumstances, you can still accept checks that people can write using credit card accounts. You have nothing to worry about in accepting them. The money comes straight out of their credit card accounts, just as if they were getting a cash advance and sending it directly to you, with no risk of a chargeback. The only problem, of course, is that not all people with credit cards have these kinds of checks.

So, should you accept credit cards? There's no easy answer. There are definite advantages and drawbacks. For starters, the process of obtaining a credit card merchant's account can be somewhat cumbersome. You have to fill out an application (quite similar to a loan application), then, based on your credit and the dollar amount per transaction you will be processing, they will assess your situation and set up your account. There are set-up charges that can cost between

$100 and $1,000, (don't allow a bank to convince you that you must purchase a credit card swiping machine . . . how can you swipe a card from hundreds of miles away?). Aside from the start-up fees, you will have to pay fees between 2½% and 7% per transaction. Why so high? Because in general, credit card companies consider lodging to be a slightly higher risk category compared to other products, thus they charge a higher rate.

Moreover, when you accept credit cards from your renters, there is always the danger of chargebacks (although very rare). This is when someone who rents your vacation home, then claims there was some sort of problem (i.e., "the place was smaller than they said it would be," "the neighbor's barking dog ruined my vacation," etc.). They tell the credit card company they are disputing the bill. And there is a possibility you might never get paid. Therefore, if you are going to take credit cards, make sure that you have a *written* agreement, signed by the renter, to charge the credit card with all of your terms and rules clearly spelled out.

I know this sounds like a pretty dismal picture, but, on the other hand, as I said, credit cards offer a lot of convenience for your renters. Suppose you are the renter (again), and you call someone (that you saw on the Internet) who owns a property. The owners say, "Yes, I have that available. It will be $1,000 rent plus a $100 cleaning fee + 10% tax. Now, please send me a personal check for $1,210." How can you be sure that person really has a property? Or if the property is as nice as described. Maybe you're being set up for a scam. Accepting credit cards gives the renters a certain amount of comfort, a feeling that they are protected.

There are many companies that offer merchant credit card accounts. You can go to your local bank, lending institution, or even to the Internet to find them. The options are about as endless as your mortgage options. Be sure to research and find the one that best suits your needs. Another option comes from Rentors.org. They offer a merchant program that is specifically designed for vacation homeowners. This program makes credit cards a viable option for you to consider. They have painstakingly worked out deals with the banks so that accepting credit cards for a vacation rental is not considered a "high risk" transaction. The result is lower fees for you. Furthermore, the application process for this specialized merchant account has been streamlined and is much simpler than other programs. Another benefit is that they will consider rental income as part of your overall financial picture. Most other credit merchant accounts will not.

Allow me to tell you about something that happened to me. Remember when I said that we rented a place in upstate New York out of the newspaper back in Chapter 6? Well, as Paul Harvey would say, "Here, my friends, is the rest of the story."

My husband and I wanted to rent a house the week of the Fourth of July on a lake in Upstate New York. We could not find any homes listed on the Internet, so we ended up renting from the newspaper. Since we were late making our reservations, all the less expensive places were booked. We ended up spending a bit more than we had anticipated. That was OK. We were even a little excited to have a nicer place. We live in Atlanta, however, and the rental house was in New York, so I had no way to see the property. There were no photographs in the paper, and although I repeatedly asked the owner to send some, he never did. But the owner was a chiropractor, and I trusted him.

We arrived all excited to have a nice, relaxing vacation. We picked up the keys at his office, as instructed. He gave us directions and we were off to spend a week at the lake.

There were certain expectations we had as we drove up to the house. After all, I spoke with the owner on the phone. I asked all the right questions. I knew exactly what to expect. Sure . . . read on. First of all, we could not find the house. We kept driving back and forth until finally a neighbor came out.

When we asked her where Doctor X's house was, she pointed to this dilapidated old shack! Surely she must be mistaken. The place I rented was one of the most expensive homes listed in the paper. The place I rented was supposed to have a deep-water dock for our boat. The place I rented was supposed to have front steps! Not a ladder leading up to the door! The house looked and smelled as though it had not been occupied in 25 years. There was no boat dock, no deep water, and I kid you not, there were no stairs up to the 3-feet off-the-ground front door! There was no toaster, coffee maker, barbecue grill, TV, radio, alarm clocks, phone, or picnic table. No, no, no! This could not be! We were scammed!

We ended up turning back around and immediately drove to Doctor X's office. It was not a pretty scene. Doctor X got defensive and belligerent (in front of his patients). We actually feared a bit for our personal safety. We even threatened to call the police. In the end, we did manage to get our rent back but he would not give back our deposit. We were a thousand miles from home, and out $300. It was a holiday weekend, we had no place to stay, and our vacation was ruined!

Now imagine how differently the situation could have been handled if we charged our vacation on a credit card. We wouldn't have worried one bit about Doctor X. We would have walked right out the door the moment we felt uncomfortable, called our credit card company and gotten *all* of our money back. So, as you can see, credit cards not only give the owners the assurance of payments, they also give the renters a certain amount of comfort, a feeling that they are protected. A very necessary feeling when you are blindly renting from strangers via the Internet. In fact, I am certain that there are some people who limit their search only to properties that accept credit cards because of this fear. You might not want to miss out on these folks' business.

Wire Transfers

One other payment method that people sometimes want to use is a wire transfer. Let me make this one as clear as possible: do not give out your personal account number for the money to be wired to. Instead, call your bank or a wire transfer location (most major grocery stores have this service), and they will have a general account number that you can have the money wired to. Giving somebody you don't know your bank account number is never a good idea. Keep in mind, with wire transfers, both the sender and the receiver are charged a transaction fee. So be sure to consider the fee, and add this charge into your rental fees.

Payment Schedules

OK, now that we know *how* you will be paid, it's time to move on to a discussion of *when* you will be paid. The key to scheduling payments is to make sure you receive your money (including deposits and fees) well in advance of the date when your guests begin renting your property. Don't worry, there is usually plenty of time to accomplish this. For example, in January, I am taking bookings for July, leaving ample time for the payments to come in.

Here is how I handle this issue. First, I require that they send me a deposit check right away, within three to five business days of the booking (and this is regardless of how far in advance they make the booking—even if it is a year in advance). Meanwhile, until you receive the deposit check—and it clears—keep taking inquiries about booking those same dates. Be honest, tell the callers there is a pending booking, but request their contact information in case there is an opening. Or, perhaps you could interest them in a different date. This happens quite frequently. In fact, in my experience, I have ended up with a large number of bookings through this exact scenario.

For a deposit, I require at least $200. I would suggest that as minimum. You will have to determine the actual number yourself, but I wouldn't recommend going over $600. Whatever number you choose, this initial deposit is critical. Be sure to cash it as soon as it arrives. If it bounces, that's a sure sign of trouble. This is your first exchange of money, and already there's a problem. Why? Call them, and ask for an explanation. If it is some sort of simple mistake (i.e., maybe they sent a check from the wrong account), you might want to ask them to send another check to cover it (along with any fees your bank charged you for the bounce). If they are cooperative, things might still work out with this renter. If not, find another renter.

Here are a few other things to remember when it comes to deposits. Do not return the deposit until after they have finished renting your property *and* you (or your maid or whomever you appoint) have had the opportunity to inspect the premises and make sure there are no damages. Only then will you return the deposit to your guests. Keep in mind (and you will have to check on this with an attorney or an accountant) that some states will require that you hold the deposit money in a separate, interest bearing escrow account. Be sure to comply with this law if it is applicable in the state in which you rent. If you accept credit cards, you have it much easier. You never have to write a refund check; just a simple transaction will credit the account.

Let me add a word here about refunds. If a person calls up, even two days after you receive his deposit check, and says something like, "I've had an illness in my family, we have to cancel. Please refund the deposit money I sent you," tell them, "OK, we'll get it in the mail to you soon." Do *not* send them the refund until their check clears your bank. Although I don't want you to get paranoid, believe it or not there are some sick people out there who try to rip you off by sending you a bad check, then getting a refund from you (with your *good* check). Don't be a victim. Yes, the guy is probably telling the truth, and there most likely is indeed an illness in his family. But waiting just a few days to get his refund (while their check clears) is not going to hurt him. As I always say, better to be safe than sorry.

Let's move on. Assuming everything works out well with the deposit, you will want to set up a payment schedule for your renters. There are number of ways you can do this, but I will share with you my own method. Here is a typical bill:

```
Thank you for choosing our condominium for your vaca-
tion. We hope that you have a pleasant stay. The unit
is located in the XYZ complex at 12345 Scenic Drive,
unit #6789, Your City, State, 23456 Phone 234-456-678.

Your confirmation is as follows:

Check-in date: June 12, 2004 after 3 P.M. CST
    (No early check-in please)

Checkout date: June 19, 2004 by 10 A.M. CST

Number of people in party: 6 adults, 2 children

Today's date: _____

After I receive your $200 deposit, your bill is as follows:

Total bill $1,581.75 = $1,350 (rental rate) +
    $75 (cleaning fee) + $156.75(11% Florida Tax)

1st payment of $790.87 due April 10, 2004 (60 days prior)

2nd payment of $790.88 due May 29, 2004 (14 days prior)

As soon as I receive your final payment, I will send/
call the lock box/key instructions.

Please sign and return 1 copy of this confirmation,
and 1 copy of the rules.

Signature_____ Date_____
```

As you see, I typically break it into at least two equal payments unless it is a last-minute reservation, then I would ask for full payment.

You should receive the first payment about 60 days prior to the rental date, this will give you ample time to get another renter if for some reason they change their mind and don't send in the payment. The balance should be paid 14–30 days prior to the rental date. This will provide plenty of time for the check to clear before you send them the key. Remember, the more time you give yourself, the more flexibility you have with payments. With enough time, you could even break it into six payments (which might be preferable for some of your guests).

Before leaving this topic, let me add a few words about long-term and last-minute guests. First, long-term. These are typically "snowbirds," older people escaping the cold, stormy weather of the Northern states who will rent for most or all of the winter. These could also be people who are taking advantage of the lower prices and will rent for an entire month during the off-season. You should require that people in these situations pay you even earlier in advance, 90 days before the rental date, because if they back out, they will be that much harder to replace. On the subject of last-minute guests (sometimes a necessity, especially if there has been a last-minute cancellation), please realize that this is a unique circumstance and you will have to adjust your normal procedures to accommodate it. For this situation, credit cards or PayPal are the ideal payment methods because you don't have to wait for payments or for the check to clear. If they're not using a credit card, do *not* accept a personal check. There might not be sufficient time for it to clear. Make an exception to your general practice and require that the funds be paid via a certified check.

These procedures work. I've been using them successfully for many years. Yes, you may come up with some minor modifications as you begin doing it yourself, but if you follow the basics outlined above, getting paid will be something you look forward to rather than a chore that you dread.

13

Collect and Pay Sales Tax

I know what you're thinking as soon as you begin reading this chapter: "Wait a minute! I never signed on to be a tax collector!" Well, rest assured, this part of the business is not as ominous as it may sound at first. Let me begin by saying that we are speaking about *sales tax*, not income tax. As a matter of fact, you've probably noticed that I don't speak much about income taxes. That's because I do not know much about them. As I said earlier, I am not an accountant. Once you own an investment property, your income taxes become more complex. Those do-it-yourself tax programs (yes, even the ones that swear they will make everything oh-so-simple) are not the best for your business. Since buying my first property, I have had an accountant file my taxes for me, and I recommend you do the same. It is money well spent.

But you do not need an accountant to help you with collecting and paying sales taxes. Sales tax on vacation rentals is required by most states though not all of them. Be sure to check with your city, county, and state sales tax departments to see if it's required in your area (see Appendix 5 for state sales tax department websites). These taxes can be called a variety of names (sales tax, tourist development tax, transient rental tax, bed tax, chamber's tax, visitors bureau tax, accommodation tax, etc.), but to you the owner, the collector, they all mean the same thing. You must collect and pay sales tax. No sense fussing over it. That's the law, so it's best that you have a solid knowledge of how it works.

For starters, understand that the money does not come from you; it comes from the renters. You are just a middleman for the government. Actually, you should look at it as a duty that ultimately works in your favor. These taxes pay for many things that are directly beneficial to your investment such as roads, sidewalks, beach preservation, and the local chamber of commerce (which is responsible for national tourism advertising campaigns; you know, those colorful, glitzy TV ads that show what a beautiful place your state is). That is why I view these taxes as a good thing. When I give seminars in Florida, the county departments of revenue always attend. I give them a chance to speak with the owners and explain how to file the taxes. They also go into great detail about what the current local taxes are allocated for. The counties *like* the tourists as much as we owners do. For the counties, sales tax brings in revenue, jobs, and growth. For us, the owners, these taxes go toward things that directly impact our property values. How is that? Well, the tax revenues give the counties the funding to make major capital improvements in the area. For example, last year, Walton County, Florida built a five- or six-mile boardwalk right in front of my condo complex. This has made the area safe for walking, jogging, and biking. Moreover, they purchased a trolley to transport renters from off-beach properties to the beach. This cuts down on traffic and congestion in front of my unit. And, they purchased dune buggies for the police department to patrol the beaches. All of these things directly impact the tourism in the area and subsequently improve my property values. So if you view the sales tax as a benefit for yourself, maybe that will make it easier to collect and pay. Remember, *somebody* has to pay for all of those things the municipality provides to make a more pleasant environment. It may as well be the renter. Be glad this is a cost you are simply passing on, and not something taken directly out of your own pocket!

If I have not yet convinced you that sales taxes are good for you, let me remind you again . . . it's the law! There are stiff fines, penalties, and interest penalties if you do not comply. Many states are beginning to come down hard on vacation property owners who are tax avoiders (I don't like to say "tax evaders," sounds too much like you can end up in prison). Please don't be naive and ask, how are they going to find out? The tax departments aren't stupid. They know about the Internet. They have people on their staff that regularly and systematically search through the listings. So, if you have a listing on the Web, the tax department will find you, eventually. I don't think I'm being overly dramatic when I say, "Big Brother is watching."

Here's the good news. Sales taxes are not difficult to file. Some states require monthly filing and others allow quarterly. It takes five minutes to fill out and file the necessary paperwork. Even a busy person, such as yourself, can handle that! Basically, it's a short form where you write in your property address, tax ID number (each tax department will assign you one), your gross rental revenue, how many days the property was occupied, and the amount of taxes you collected. This is a very simple formula. It does *not* take an accounting agree, just a calculator. You even get to keep a 2%–3% tax allowance! (That's 2%–3% of the sales tax collected, *not* your gross revenue). The only difficult part of filing is remembering to do it each month or quarter. You can set up an automatic reminder on your computer, or simply make a note on the appropriate date on your calendar.

OK, so I now have you convinced to collect and pay sales tax, but what exactly is taxable? You charge a separate cleaning fee, as well as other fees. Are those fees taxable? Please realize that each governing office may have different rules regarding this so be sure to check with your tax offices. Here's my interpretation. Most sales tax laws say that any fees associated as part of the rental agreement are taxable, meaning any money that you keep. Cleaning fees, if they are charged as an extra fee associated with the rental, are taxable. But your maid should not be charging you tax on her services. That is double taxation. Also, if you charge a pet fee that you keep, that's taxable too. But deposits, including pet deposits that are returned, are *not* taxable since they are being returned, even if there are damages, and you have to withhold money from the deposit. While you certainly don't want to short change the government, make sure you don't cheat yourself out of money either.

For example, if you charge $1,000 per week + $75 cleaning fee + $200 refundable deposit, then $1,075 is taxable (the rental rate + cleaning fee) and the $200 is not taxable (since this is just a security deposit that will be refunded). Now, if you charge $1,000 per week + $75 cleaning fee + $200 refundable deposit + $300 pet fee, then the taxable amount is $1,375 (the rental rate + cleaning fee + pet fee). However, if you charge $1,000 per week + $75 cleaning fee + $200 refundable deposit + $300 pet *deposit* (refundable), then the taxable amount is only $1,075 since the $200 and $300 charges are *refundable*. Keep in mind that taxes are charged on anything associated with rental, so if you require that they pay per bundle of firewood, for use of your fishing boat, use of a snowmobile, etc., those charges are taxable.

Now what about snowbirds and monthly rentals? Do you have to charge sales tax for these long-term rentals? Most states require more than six months rental in order for it to be considered non-transient. However this is another regulation that varies from state to state. In most cases, you will also have to provide a bona fide written lease for that state's minimum amount of months, along with specific terms. Be sure to check with your local tax office before you tell any renter that you will not have to charge sales tax.

As I said, I think collecting sales taxes is relatively easy. Still, some of you may not want to go through the hassles of setting up your sales tax accounts and/or filing returns monthly or quarterly. Well, you'll be glad to know that there is a service you can hire to do this for you. HotSpotManagement.com, specifically created for vacation property owners, will set up your tax accounts and file all the necessary forms and taxes for you. After all, your mother always dreamed you would be a doctor, *not a tax collector.*

14

Handling Keys

You live in Indiana, your renters live in Texas, and your property is in Colorado. How do you get the keys to the renters? Don't worry, this is not as complicated as it seems.

You have many options when it comes to keys. First, you can use the old-fashioned method of mailing the keys to your renters. Many owners have been doing this for twenty or thirty or more years. When my husband and I first got married, we used to vacation at Martha's Vineyard every year. We rented directly from an owner. She would mail us the keys before we left, and then we would mail them back after we returned. It was effective. Effective, but not necessarily simple. You may not have given it much thought, but mailing keys leaves a lot of room for error. And it means more work than is really necessary. The problem is you have to make numerous sets of keys, send them out in a timely manner so that your renter receives them before they leave home, and then you have to be sure that your renters mail the keys back to you. Forget any one of these steps and you will have a potentially serious problem on your hands. What if the renters forget to bring the keys with them when they leave your rental home? What if they don't send them back? What if they lose them while they are there?

I think that the best way to alleviate all this trouble is to drop the idea of mailing keys and go with your second option: buy a combination key box. A key box attaches to your doorknob or somewhere on your property. The most common ones are made by GE, are very inexpensive ($25–$30), and can be found at most hardware stores, from locksmiths, or on the Internet (just a note: there are many brands out there, but I like the three-key portable push button made by GE. It holds up to the elements quite well, and I have used the same one for many years). A key box is not a complex piece of equipment. You easily set your own code, hang it on your doorknob, and put the keys inside the box. You then give the renter the combination when you send them the driving directions (they usually don't forget the directions when they leave home, and even if they do, you could always give them the code over the phone). The key box combination is easy to change, but the downside is that you have to be there physically to do it.

Your third option is to buy some sort of keyless entry door lock. These are similar to what you see in most banks and offices. The kind that has push buttons right on the locks. These locks are great but they are pretty expensive ($200–$600). They can also be found online or through most locksmiths and hardware stores. You might also want to consider the newest type of keyless lock, the kind that offers remote access. Again, these are pretty pricey, but they do offer many conveniences such as the ability to store, change, and create combinations from your home computer or even via cell phone. The downside (besides price) is that they are electronic, and most use batteries. Anything electronic can malfunction and the batteries, although they usually last three years, can go dead. These types of locks also have a monthly service fee associated with them. So why tell you about them? Because for many owners, this may be the only option (aside from mailing keys). There are many condominium complexes that prohibit lock boxes. Even realtors are not allowed to use them. These complexes most likely have an on-site rental management company. I doubt very much that these companies will hand out your keys to your guests (since you are now a competitor!).

Lost Keys

You get the phone call, the one you knew was inevitable one of these days: "We went to the beach, a big wave hit, and I lost my keys." What do you do if your renters lose their keys? Well, if you decide to purchase one of the keyless locks, this will not be a problem for you. But if you use either of the other two methods, then you will *most likely* have this happen eventually. The best way to solve this is to prepare ahead of time. Be proactive. The most logical solution is to turn to your maid for lost key issues (see, I told you they are your lifelines!). Set up fees and protocol ahead of time. Will your maid want your renters to call her directly, or should they call you first? Ahh, now you're thinking, if they locked themselves out, and your phone number and the maid's number are inside the unit, then how will they call? You see, I am very crafty and have thought of every angle (actually, I got burned once, and I learned from my mistake). Simply put a sticker inside the lock box with your contact numbers on it. This way, since the lock box always stays on the door, they can open it and retrieve this information. Also consider your maid and fees. If she has to come out to help renters, how much would she want for her services? During regular business hours, after hours, or in the middle of the night? Be sure that these fees are on your rental rules.

Next, you should distribute your keys to everyone you can. This way, if your maid is unavailable, you are still covered. Give keys to other owners, association managers, maybe even the realtor who sold you the place.

Now, the next thing you should do is hide a key somewhere. If you have a single family dwelling, this is very easy to do. You can even purchase a second lock box, put a different code on it and mount it in a more obscure place (this is good for maintenance people too, since you're giving a different code than your regular lock box code that the renters use). Of course, if you own a condominium, you'll have to be a little more creative. After my first incident when my guests were locked out, I became very inventive:

It was Fourth of July weekend. I was in upstate New York dealing with the property that my family and I rented for the week after finding it in the newspaper. My cell phone rang, and it was my maid in Florida. She had an accident and was in the hospital (thankfully not badly injured). She was not going to be able to clean my condo. And, of course, I had guests due to arrive in just a few hours. My first thought was oh no, but then I remembered that I am a proactive owner! I have a back-up maid. I called the back-up maid, and she just happened to be at the unit downstairs. No problem, she'll clean my place too. I hung up and thought, good . . . solved. About an hour later, my back-up maid called to tell me that her key does not fit my door. My blood pressure shot through the ceiling! I forgot to give her a key the last time I changed the locks. But again, I had a solution. "No problem, here's my lock box code," I said, "The keys are inside." She called back two minutes later. "Christine, I got the lock box open, and there are no keys inside." By that point, my blood pressure must have been off the chart. My renters either forgot to put the keys inside the lock box, or they left them in the unit. Now what? I thought and thought, then . . . an epiphany! I told her to go upstairs to another owner's unit. I gave her that unit's lock box code. I told her to go inside and go to the utility closet. I told her to feel the backside of the hot water tank (I'm sure she thought I was nuts!). Taped to the backside of the hot water tank was a key to my unit! Luckily, I had remembered to replace that one when I changed the locks. The back-up maid entered my unit and was able to clean my unit before the next guest arrived. Disaster averted.

Liability with Keys

I know that a concern with many owners is the liability associated with keys. First and foremost, be sure that whoever you give your keys to is trustworthy. Do *not* put the address or unit number on any key, especially hidden keys. Also, on your lock boxes, since you cannot change your codes after each renter, be sure explain to each renter, in writing (on the directions is good place to do so), that the code is not changed after each checkout. Tell them not to use the lock box as a holding spot for the keys while they go out.

As an owner, you must install, in addition to your regular lock, some type of keyless lock on the inside of the unit. This can either be an old-fashioned chain or a keyless dead bolt. This is for the safety of the people inside. You would not want anyone to be able to use a key and come inside and harm your guests.

Another important task you must do is re-key your locks (at least once a year). The best method to re-key the locks is to take the locks off the doors and take them to your local hardware store and for around ten dollars you can them re-keyed. This is also good for your locks because when they re-key, they typically take apart the lock, clean and lubricate it, which prevents your locks from keys getting stuck or not working at all.

Like so many issues associated with vacation home rentals, the important thing to remember about keys is that a little bit of planning goes a long way toward avoiding future problems. Just think of me and my maid story. The only reason it had a happy ending was because I had built what NASA would call "redundancy" into my system. When they send a spacecraft millions of miles away from Earth, what if something goes wrong? They solve this problem by building backup systems that cover for any equipment that fails. Think about keys in much the same way. After all, though you're not millions of miles away, you may well be *hundreds* of miles away—bad enough. Of course, a backup system for keys is much easier than fixing a probe sent into deep space, and you don't need to be a rocket scientist.

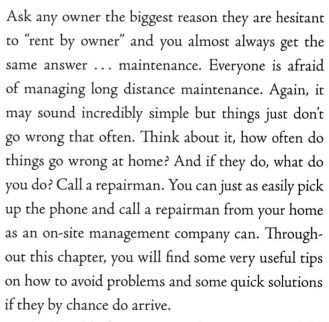

CHAPTER

15

Cleaning and Maintenance

Ask any owner the biggest reason they are hesitant to "rent by owner" and you almost always get the same answer ... maintenance. Everyone is afraid of managing long distance maintenance. Again, it may sound incredibly simple but things just don't go wrong that often. Think about it, how often do things go wrong at home? And if they do, what do you do? Call a repairman. You can just as easily pick up the phone and call a repairman from your home as an on-site management company can. Throughout this chapter, you will find some very useful tips on how to avoid problems and some quick solutions if they by chance do arrive.

As I said before, your maid service is your lifeline. It is vital. Remember my nightmare that a renter will show up and find the place dirty? Sure, you could have your renters clean the property themselves, but you are giving up control of your home when you do this. Is that something you really want to do? After all, your idea of clean may not be the same as mine. The "clean it yourself" system seems to only work in cottages and cabins when the renters are required to bring all their own bedding and linens. Even then, the owners are generally not too satisfied with the cleanliness ... and you certainly cannot go and clean your home every time a renter leaves! That leaves you with hiring *somebody* or some *company*.

Well, you know the old cliché: good help is hard to find. So just how do you find a maid? You're probably not expecting this answer—literally right outside your front door! Visit your property on a weekend and go outside when most renters are usually checking out. I can almost guarantee that your neighbors have cleaning services. Now don't be a stranger. Talk to the people cleaning; ask who they work for. Even if your neighbor uses a management company, these workers are usually willing to pick up a side job. What if the maid you talk to would love to work for you but does not have time? Consider staggering your checkout time so that she can clean both. Remember, you are in control. Take advantage of that. There's no rule that says checkout must be 10 A.M. and check-in must be 3 P.M. Don't rule out the maids that are cleaning your place currently through your management company. If he or she is a subcontractor, not an actual employee, you can possibly hire him or her. It's definitely worth looking into.

Another good, yet overlooked, resource for maids is your local church. Sometimes a pastor will know of someone who is looking for extra work. It pays to be resourceful. Don't give up on the idea of hiring an individual just because "it's impossible to find good help these days." No, it's not impossible. Don't believe that old cliché.

The next question almost always seems to be, should I hire an individual or should I hire a company? I wish there was an easy answer, but there are benefits and potential problems with both. Cleaning services do tend to be more reliable in the sense that yes, they will show up consistently. Because they have multiple crews of employees, if/when someone is out, there is another person to pick up the slack. But the downside is you'll have different people cleaning your place each week, which means they don't have a chance to become familiar with the property. Also, large cleaning services work in volume and tend not to take as much time taking care of your individual needs. They generally have a set list of duties they perform, and they tend not to deviate from that list. An upside is that cleaning services are easily found because they are listed in the phonebook and other directories. Most times, cleaning services are less expensive than individuals.

Individuals, on the other hand, usually take more time to clean and pay attention to details and your specific requests. Most will even do light maintenance such as change light bulbs, change furnace filters, and add personal touches. They also tend to be better at communicating with you about your unit.

I have tried both and have just had better luck with individuals. But, as I've said, the right person can be hard to find. Regardless of which you choose, you should always have names and contact information for back-up in case you get into a situation where your cleaning service does not show up.

Be sure to have a list of expectations for your cleaning posted somewhere inside your unit. The back of a closet door works well. Don't worry about hiding it from view of your renters, it's OK for them to see that you have high expectations for your cleaning staff. It will make them even more certain that they made the right choice in renting your home.

Now . . . maintenance. Don't put the book down! This isn't going to hurt. Proper maintenance is imperative, so you just have to be sure to go about it the right way. Remember, this is the thing that's either going to make your rentals run smoothly or make your life hell. Do not view this as your primary residence. By that I mean, when was the last time you had service in your home? Most likely when something was broken. Well, just put aside the old way of thinking, "if it ain't broke don't fix it." With your vacation property, I advocate the exact opposite. You must do preventative maintenance on *everything* that you possibly can. I almost hesitate to say it because I know you've heard it countless times as a kid . . . but it bears repeating, so I'll say it again: an ounce of prevention is worth a pound of cure.

You need to try to anticipate all of your problems up front and fix them before they become an issue. This is where you'll really come to view vacation property ownership as a business venture. Don't get worked up about spending $75 twice a year to have your furnace cleaned. Remember all the money you are saving from not having a management company? It's OK to spend some of it here. What is that $75 compared to all the money you're saving. I promise it will make your life easier.

Furthermore, you can hire a maintenance person to oversee your property. This works particularly well for people who live very far from their second home and for those who don't have time to visit more than once or twice a year. The good news is that maintenance people are much easier to find than maids, and you can use the same tactics that you used to find your maids. There are companies and individuals that you can hire. They can do as little or as much as you feel you need. Some people have a maintenance person come to their property each time a guest leaves to check on things such as light bulbs, furnace filters, leaky faucets, etc. Others choose to have their maids police the needs and notify you/or your maintenance person if there is a problem. It's your property and your choice. Experiment a little and find out what works best for you.

Don't overlook the fact that your neighbors are also renting. You may be able to pool your resources and find someone you can all hire together. Condominium complexes usually have on-staff maintenance. Check with the complex maintenance person and see if he or she would like to moonlight. One condominium complex where I own has so many self-managing owners (I taught many of them) that the association was able to hire one full-time maintenance person to work for the owners, and each owner simply pays on an hourly basis. Read what this resourceful owner did:

> Ed and his wife live in New York. They own a vacation property on Grand Cayman Island. Ed saw the benefits of renting by owner because a lot of his neighbors were doing it. Ed was apprehensive about joining them, however, because of the maintenance aspect of rentals. After all, how was he supposed to fix anything from New York? Ed came up with an ingenious solution to this problem. Now you must understand that Grand Cayman does have high-season and low-season rates, but most properties are booked 40+ weeks per year. So their rental revenue was quite high, but so were the management commissions. Since there were six other people who were renting by owner, Ed decided that they could band together and hire one person to oversee maintenance for all their properties. He figured that they could hire one full-time person, and each owner would pay two months of this person's salary. When other owners in the complex heard what these six owners were doing, they also were very interested. In the end, the 12 owners agreed to each pay one month of the maintenance person's salary. They now have a full-time employee, devoted to maintaining their 12 units, and the satisfaction of renting by owner, without all the worries.

As for me, I am a "by owner" purist. I do it all. Remember, if you follow my book, you will be renting to "friends." For the most part, I don't get calls for little things. Your renters will do quick-solve maintenance themselves, and you'll most likely never even hear about it. Now I am *not* advocating that you have your renters do maintenance for you. You still have to do all of your preventative maintenance up front. For example, I've never gotten a call for a stopped up toilet. No,

I don't have a special clog proof toilet, but I do have a plunger, and I think that the renters just use it. They know I live 400 miles away, so they don't call me for minor maintenance. Other issues such as a broken washing machine, electrical problems, or a leak from the upstairs unit (all of which have happened to me) are the real hurdles. In these cases, I simply call a repairperson. I keep a copy of the area phonebook at my home. The renters, or my cleaning service, let the repairperson into my unit and the work gets done. Yes, it is an inconvenience for your renters but they are almost always very understanding about these things, and the bottom line is these problems do not happen all that often. When the day is done, I compensate them for their inconvenience by either refunding a portion of the rent or taking a percentage off their next stay.

Here's another story that you may find instructive:

Mike and Michelle own a cabin in the Pennsylvania mountains, and they live in New Jersey. They rented their cabin to a family with children. One night, they got a phone call from the renters. It seems that their son had been leaning back in his chair (we've all seen this before) and fell back. The boy was fine, but the chair put a small hole in the wall. The father told Mike that he noticed that there was some drywall spackle under the sink. He was calling to ask if it was all right if he just fixed the hole himself. He also wanted to know if there was some touch up paint somewhere.

To which I say, don't you just love a happy ending? Seriously, there's a great lesson to this story. You see, often when we think about maintenance, we assume that we are just talking about appliances, plumbing, and other such basics. But in reality, more often than not things go wrong because the renters themselves have damaged something, almost always by mistake. Most renters will be responsible and conscientious about the damages they have caused. And, given the proper tools, most would rather just fix or solve the problem themselves. What must have been going through this dad's mind? If I were him, the first thing that I would think is how much is this going to cost us? Especially if it's something I can just fix myself. Renters don't want to get socked with damage charges as much as you don't want the damages.

Below you will find a list of things that you can do to your property for preventative maintenance, as well as items you should have on hand for those accidental damages. Give the renters the chance to fix the problems on their own. Sounds obvious, right? Maybe. Or maybe not. Let me share with you an example from my own experience.

> I was at my condo in Florida last summer. Halfway through the week, my son came in, and said, "Mom, my teacher is here!" We just happened to be vacationing in the same place at the same time. I went out and began talking to her. After a while she said, "Christine, can I ask you a favor? Can I borrow your broom?" She was renting a place on the beach that did not have a broom! How could she as a renter possibly keep it clean? The sand! I was astonished!

Let's take a look at that list. Be sure everything is in working order (especially advertised items), and keep good records of all maintenance. Here are the essentials:

+ Keep a copy of the local phonebook for your vacation property in your permanent home so you can easily find appropriate maintenance contractors.
+ Write down make, model, and serial numbers of all major appliances. If you need to schedule service, you can have this information on hand.
+ Consider purchasing extended warrantees on major appliances, especially washers and dryers, since they are appliances that are used above and beyond normal.

- Have your dryer vent cleaned regularly. Or when you visit, take your leaf blower and blow it out yourself.
- Clean the condenser coils on your refrigerator.
- Have your furnace/air conditioner cleaned and checked regularly.
- Change furnace filters at least once a month.
- Schedule regular chimney and fireplace cleaning and inspections. General rule of thumb is after each cord of wood burned.
- Clean out the screens on your faucets and showerheads, especially with wells and hard water areas.
- For properties using wells, consider replacing water consumption appliances with water saving appliances (i.e., toilets, front load washing machines, dishwashers, shower heads).
- Clean out sink/drains regularly. Hair is the most common cause of slow and clogged drains. To do this, unscrew the stopper in sinks and bathtubs and clean out the hair.
- Consider installing a kitchen sink disposal.
- Inspect breaker panels and plug receptacles at least once every two years, especially in salt-water areas. Salt corrodes wiring and causes malfunctions.
- Schedule regular pest control.
- In areas where rodents and pests are a problem, regularly check property for point of entry and plug those areas. These are sometimes included in pest control contracts but be sure it's being done.
- Schedule regular landscape maintenance and snow removal.
- Schedule regular carpet cleaning, or consider installing ceramic, hard wood, or solid surface flooring.
- Schedule a deep cleaning at least once a year, including washing throw rugs, curtains and blinds, ovens, baseboards, and steam clean sofas, etc.
- Wash all blankets and comforters at least once every 10 rentals.

- Replace things often before they get worn out and dingy, especially coffee makers, toasters, blenders, wash cloths, towels, pillows, and all bedding.
- Set up storm policies with a maid or maintenance person. Have them do whatever is necessary to storm-proof your property for example, pull in patio furniture, turn off appliances, etc.
- For owners who close their property for the winter, schedule maintenance person or maid to check up on your property during the closed season.

Maintenance Supplies

Be sure to have these items on hand:
- Broom, mop, and vacuum.
- Cleaning supplies, including window cleaner and bleach or disinfectant.
- Plungers near each toilet.
- Shovel and ice melt, sand or salt.
- Spackle and trowel.
- Touch-up paint (in a small jar clearly marked), paintbrush, or disposable sponge brush.
- Hammer, screwdrivers (flat head and Phillips head), nails and screws, pliers, channel locks, crescent wrench. These tools can be found at dollar stores.
- Teflon tape for quick plumbing repairs.
- A tube of silicone.
- Wood glue.
- Liquid drain opener.
- Extra batteries for smoke detectors and TV remotes.
- Light bulbs, in all sizes and wattage's including appliance bulbs.
- Duct tape (there are millions of uses).
- Extra furnace filters

I'm betting you can think of many other items you might want to add to this list, but I think you get the idea. Maintenance is not the nightmare subject you thought it was. Things just don't go wrong that often. Unless, of course, you don't prepare for it. Then all bets are off.

CHAPTER
16

Furnishings and Supplies

Here's an important question: why do people rent vacation homes rather than just stay in a hotel? There are numerous reasons, but I can tell you that convenience is a big part of it. Not only will they have a kitchen, but also they will have furnishings and other amenities that you just won't find in a standard hotel room. In other words, they will feel right at home. So how you furnish your vacation home will make a big difference to your guests. It may be a critical factor in their decision to return next year. They may even tell their friends what a gem they have found and suggest they should try it out too.

Let's start with the kitchen. There is nothing more annoying to a renter than an ill-equipped kitchen. Conversely, I cannot tell you how many times my guests have complimented my well-equipped kitchen. When furnishing your kitchen, be sure to have ample supplies on hand for your renters. The general rule of thumb is have at least double the amount of dishes, cups, glasses, etc., that your property sleeps. So if you sleep 8, have dishes for 16. This serves a couple of purposes. First, it's for the convenience of the renter, especially when they're on vacation. People don't like having to take the dishes they used for breakfast out of the dishwasher and hand wash them to eat lunch.

Secondly, having enough dishes and utensils will conserve water and power. They'll only run the dishwasher when it's full, not because they need a clean plate. Also consider supplying a set of dishwasher safe, hard plastic cups, especially if you have a pool or hot tub. Another thing that renters appreciate is little plastic cups, bowls and plates, for little children (and this will also help alleviate spills). Don't overlook the utensils, gadgets, and appliances that are specific to your particular area. If you're on the beach, for example, a big lobster pot and lobster/crab crackers are essential. And if you're in a colder climate, a crock-pot and recipes for your favorite soups or stews would be a nice thing to have.

You also want be sure to furnish your unit in an appropriate manner. By this I mean don't put satin sheets in a cabin that is mainly rented by men's hunting groups, and don't use a plastic outdoor patio set as your dining room table in a place that rents for $3,000 a week. There are certain levels of comfort and furnishings that renters expect in specific markets and price points. Do the best to make your place feel homey and welcoming, not stuffy or sparsely decorated. The importance of family photos is often overlooked. Adding your family photos gives your property the personalized feel that renters are looking for. It's also a good deterrent for damages and theft. I once had a friend stay at my place, and she told me she turned my photo upside down. She said she felt as though I was watching her. My response was, "Good!"

When you are purchasing furnishings, keep in the back of your mind that you are renting this property. Spend your money wisely.

Take into consideration that you will need to replace furnishings more often than you do at home. You might buy the best quality furnishings for your home, but I wouldn't for a rental unit. I prefer less expensive, lesser quality furniture, not the bottom of the barrel, however. I simply plan on replacing them more often. I could spend $3,000 for a sofa that's great quality and looks nice, or I can spend $1,000 for one that looks nice but is only of decent quality. I can replace that one three times for the same amount as the top of the line.

With some items, of course, it is necessary to have the best quality. Kitchen and dining room chairs are the first things that come to mind. I am a relatively small person, so I never thought about this. The first place I owned had nice looking, medium quality chairs. I found that within a couple of years, most of them had broken. Some people are very hard on chairs. And face it, some people are pretty heavy. I recommend all chairs (interior and exterior) have a 300-pound capacity. There are many styles of wrought iron interior dining sets available these days. I highly recommend them.

One mistake some people make is to just put all their old furnishing from their home into their rental units and get new stuff for home. But your renters may not necessarily want that old stuff either. So consider bringing it to your local charity and taking a write-off instead. I have used an occasional old piece of furniture here and there, but never without refinishing it or a giving it a nice coat of paint or faux finish. Don't fill your house with your treasured family heirlooms either. Since some people may not remember that coaster under their frosty glass of lemonade, I recommend you purchase glass to cover the tops of wooden dining room and bedside tables.

As for beds, make sure they are firm or extra firm. Comfortable beds are very important. One compromise that renters will rarely make is on bed size. Ask any hotel which rooms are the first to fill up. The answer is always the king-size rooms. If renters have a king-size bed at home, then chances are they will have a tough time sleeping on anything smaller. If one of your bedrooms can accommodate a king-size bed, I highly recommend you purchase one.

Decorating your second home can be a lot of fun. Mine is decorated nicer than my residence! But I caution you here. It is so easy to get caught up buying too much décor for your vacation home. Avoid that cluttered look. When the renter looks in, as they scan, their first impression is very important. If they see a lot of stuff, the first impression may be that the place is cluttered or not clean. Be sure to give the right impression. Whatever you do, do not over decorate.

Also, I know that they are cute, but those nice wooden model sailboats are too much of a temptation for little hands. Keep in mind when you are decorating, there will most likely be a child occupying the rooms. Glass top coffee tables are durable and look nice, but I shutter to think of the toddler who falls onto the corner of it. Plug covers and safety locks on cabinets should also not be overlooked. And you might want to add a highchair and porta-crib. I do not recommend you supply car seats. Be careful when supplying any items for infants and small children, as baby items are the number one manufacturer-recalled items (mainly for safety issues).

There are certain safety considerations that you should keep in mind when furnishing your property. Some states even require periodic safety inspections. Check with your state sales tax office, they can tell you if a state safety inspection is required for your property. But even if your property is not subject to a safety inspection, it is a good idea to be sure that you have working smoke detectors and fire extinguishers within easy access. You should also clearly post emergency information such as evacuation plans, poison control centers, etc. As an added safety measure, purchase automatic shut off irons and coffee makers. You may also include first aid kits, and appropriate warnings about area wildlife dangers (raccoons, bears, snakes, jellyfish, ticks, etc.).

On my directions to my renters, I always write: "Keep your eyes open if on the beach at dusk or dawn. We often see dolphins swimming right off shore. If the dolphins come in close, which they do occasionally, do not get in the water, and try to touch them. Please respect the wildlife; it is illegal to touch the dolphins. We humans have germs that harm the dolphins."

Besides furnishing your vacation home with the obvious items that renters expect, there are also things you can add that will just make it a more enjoyable place to be. Things that show that you have put a lot of thought and personal attention into your home. I am a true believer that every vacation property needs to have relaxing family activities on hand. These things include videos, DVDs, CDs, books, magazines, and games (Yahtzee, Scrabble, and a deck of playing cards are a *must*). If your property is near the beach, other fun activity items might include sand buckets and sand shovels. This will also stop the kids from using your kitchen utensils as digging tools! Then, there are a various assortment of bathroom items that you can include, such as blow dryers, shampoo, soap, razors, etc. Even extra hats and mittens from the dollar store would be greatly appreciated by that skier who loses his on the slopes.

The next question that seems to follow this advice is: do these things get stolen? For the most part, these items are not stolen. People appreciate these extras. But don't spend thousands filling your place with things that will be a temptation. Many of these odds and ends can be purchased at the dollar store or at second-hand stores. I have had people take things home, but, believe it or not, they mail them back, or they call and say, "We took this home by mistake." There's more honesty out there than you may realize.

One of the most appreciated items in my property is something that cost next to nothing to supply. I created my own guidebook. I bought a three-ring binder and some blank clear plastic sleeves. I filled it with all sorts of area attractions, restaurant menus, church schedules, directions to grocery stores, and coupons. I included little notes about my unit, where things can be found, how to work things, manuals for the stereo, VCR, DVD player, etc. This is also where I put information about my checkout policies. I keep a copy of my rules in there, too.

By the way, don't forget yourself! You will need a place to store your own personal things that you wouldn't necessarily want your renters to have. Set a closet aside that is designated as an owner's closet and lock it. I keep all our personal belongings in this closet so that it makes packing up and going to my vacation home a breeze. It is where I keep all of our toiletries, my personal sheets and bedding (I like my own), laundry detergent, all sorts of cleaning supplies and extra supplies for my property. I even keep some non-perishable food items there. I installed a lock on the door and always keep it locked. My maid has a key to my owner's closet, and I also hide a key in my unit.

Many owners are reluctant to take a closet away from a bedroom for this purpose. Don't be. You should make it as easy and convenient as possible for yourself too. Remember the real reason you bought this vacation home in the first place. I took a closet out of the smallest bedroom and converted into our owner's closet. Then, I purchased a wardrobe at an estate sale and placed it right in front of the closet door. This way my renters still have a place to hang their things, and I still have all my belongings for me too.

Furnishing your property is a mix of the practical and the aesthetic. A little creativity can go a long way in this department. You don't want to spend a fortune, but you do want to create an atmosphere that is warm, inviting—and safe—for your guests, and for yourself.

HIGHLY RECOMMENDED ITEMS

- ❑ 13x9 baking dish
- ❑ 2 qt. pyrex dish
- ❑ basting spoon
- ❑ broom/mop/dust pan
- ❑ can piercer/ bottle opener
- ❑ coffee pot (auto shut off)
- ❑ cookie sheet
- ❑ cutting board
- ❑ fire extinguisher
- ❑ large skillet
- ❑ lg. glass casserole dish
- ❑ measuring spoons
- ❑ med. covered saucepan
- ❑ micro/refrig. dishes
- ❑ paring knife
- ❑ roast knife
- ❑ rubber spatula
- ❑ salad serving spoons
- ❑ slotted spoon
- ❑ spatula
- ❑ toaster (wide slot)
- ❑ vegetable peeler

- ❑ 2 cake pans
- ❑ 3 pc. mixing bowls
- ❑ blender
- ❑ can opener
- ❑ coasters
- ❑ colander
- ❑ cork screw
- ❑ Dutch oven w/lid
- ❑ fondue set
- ❑ lg. covered saucepan
- ❑ lobster pot
- ❑ meat fork
- ❑ medium skillet
- ❑ microwave
- ❑ plastic pitcher
- ❑ roaster w/lid
- ❑ salad bowl
- ❑ salt/pepper shakers
- ❑ soup ladle
- ❑ tea kettle
- ❑ tongs
- ❑ hot pad/trivet

DINNERWARE

You should have twice the amount of plates, cups, etc. that your unit accommodates. If your property sleeps 4, have a service for 8, etc.

- ❑ dinner plates
- ❑ bowls
- ❑ saucers
- ❑ salad forks
- ❑ teaspoons
- ❑ steak knives
- ❑ water glasses
- ❑ wine glasses

- ❑ sandwich plates
- ❑ cups/mugs
- ❑ dinner forks
- ❑ tablespoons
- ❑ table knives
- ❑ tea glasses
- ❑ rock glasses

MISCELLANEOUS

- ❏ blankets
- ❏ mattress pads
- ❏ shower liner
- ❏ phones
- ❏ lamps
- ❏ TV (cable ready with remotes)
- ❏ plungers
- ❏ ashtrays (if applicable)
- ❏ iron (auto shut off)
- ❏ phone and phonebook
- ❏ VCR/DVD
- ❏ pillow protectors
- ❏ waste cans
- ❏ alarm clock/radio
- ❏ pictures
- ❏ pillows (two per bed including sofa bed)
- ❏ vacuum cleaner
- ❏ fly swatter
- ❏ ironing board
- ❏ CD player

OTHER ITEMS

Things that are nice to have but not necessary:

- ❏ reading lamp
- ❏ door mats
- ❏ beach chairs/service
- ❏ patio set
- ❏ basket ball hoop
- ❏ boogie boards
- ❏ volleyball net
- ❏ napkin holder
- ❏ ice-cream scoop
- ❏ hatchet
- ❏ plastic plates, cups, bowls for children
- ❏ cookbooks
- ❏ porta-crib
- ❏ plug covers
- ❏ rolling pin
- ❏ games (Yahtzee, Scrabble, cards)
- ❏ videos/DVDs
- ❏ BBQ grill and utensils
- ❏ hot tub
- ❏ tennis racquets
- ❏ bikes
- ❏ crock-pot
- ❏ rubber tub mat
- ❏ placemats
- ❏ crab/nut crackers
- ❏ dishwasher safe plastic cups
- ❏ office supplies (PC/printer/fax)
- ❏ high chair
- ❏ safety locks for cabinets
- ❏ first aid kit
- ❏ hair dryer

17

Solving Problems

UGH! This is a topic I hate talking about. Wouldn't it be wonderful if the world were full of *perfect renters?* Well, unfortunately in the real world, problems do arise. Thank goodness there are more good people in this world than bad. But you still have to be prepared for those occasional people who give you a major headache. Remember, the best way to avoid problems is to screen your guests as effectively as possible. If you get that phone call from a 40-year-old business executive who's coming for his college fraternity reunion, think twice about whether you will rent to him. That's a situation I would rather not take a chance on.

On a positive note, I can say that damages are rarely a problem, and theft is virtually unheard of. In all the years I have been renting, I have never had anything stolen from my property. I also surveyed owners on this and only found 1 out of 150 owners ever experienced any sort of theft. We have had damages, of course, but most were quite minor. Although getting through these issues is not fun, it doesn't have to be a nightmare if you handle it in a calm, professional manner.

When dealing with these difficult issues, it's imperative that you switch modes and become a businessperson. First, don't get into an argument. Keep your emotions out of it. Think of yourself as a gate agent at the airport dealing with irate customers who have just been informed that their flight has been delayed or canceled. I think gate agents are the most skilled group of customer service employees. They are always so calm. I watch them in amazement as they deal with customers. Unlike a lot of other industries, where customer service employees are trained to do whatever pleases the customer (give the meal free at a restaurant, discount a defective product, etc.), gate agents are trained to keep control of the situation without giving in to the customer's unreasonable demands. Let them be your example.

You, the owner, can control the situation without losing the upper hand. Do whatever you feel is fair and reasonable in a given situation. Remember, you only have to compensate when there is a valid reason, not because the customer demands it.

Given every potential problem, as always your best course of action is to be proactive rather than reactive. Set yourself up ahead of time with clearly defined rental rules and check-in policies. Here are some guidelines for the most common problems.

Major Damage

OK, I know that you are thinking, "I live far away. How would I even know if there were any damages to my vacation home?" This is where you need to have good communication with your cleaning staff. Instruct them to call you immediately. This is the reason for the damage or theft deposit. Keep a Polaroid or a disposable camera in your owner's locked closet along with a self-addressed stamped envelope. If there is damage, have your maid take photos and send you the pictures. Now you have proof of the damage and a way to assess the cost. It should go without saying that you will not refund the deposit until you know what is owed to you. And you certainly won't rent to them again.

I had a situation once where my renters broke my bed frame. Now a bed is something that is necessary to have for the next renter. Under this circumstance, I asked the maid to send one of her employees to the local mattress store to purchase a new frame. I told the maid I would be happy to pay that person's hourly salary. They went, bought the bed, and I sent my maid the reimbursement for her time and expenses. And I took the money out of the deposit from that renter. When I sent the unused portion of the deposit, I mailed a nice letter stating that I was keeping $71.54 of their deposit for the bed that was broken. You can also attach receipts for remedied damages. I also sent them a copy of the rental rules that they signed upon booking and highlighted the section referring to damage deposits. I never heard from them again.

Minor Damage or Theft

Should you worry about every little thing like a broken glass or lost silverware? No. You cannot micro-manage your place. In the grand scheme of things, these are just minor expenses you have to figure on as part of owning a rental property. If you're concerned, ask your renters that if they break anything, please replace it. This is much easier than collecting money and this way the items will be there for the next renter. Verbal policy for broken items—have renters replace it with equal quality them themselves.

Why am I suggesting that this be a verbal, rather than written policy? In case they break something valuable and replace it with something very inferior. For example, let's say you have a 36" TV, and it is destroyed when one of their kids throws a ball through it. Then they replace it with a 19" TV. You don't want them to take something that you put down in writing and get into a dispute over "equal quality" and use it as a justification for shortchanging you.

I always make it a practice to say something like this to my guests: "This is my second home. I live 400 miles away. I can't worry about every little broken item. If you break something that you feel the next renter would need, say the coffee pot, I would much rather you just go to Wal-Mart and buy a new one. This way I don't have to try and figure out how much to charge you (out of your deposit), and the main objective is that these things are there for every renter. If you break one plate, don't worry about it, but if you break the whole stack, be sure to replace them." I've found that most renters are quite comfortable with this policy.

Cleanliness Problems

Let's say your renters have checked out, and you get a phone call from your maid saying that your renters left the place a total mess. Beer cans everywhere, crayon on the walls, a huge stain on the carpet. Use your imagination . . . it can be pretty bad. Rather than get upset, however, remember your objective. You need to get the place ready for the people checking in later today. Do whatever it takes. If it means calling a carpet cleaner and having them come out immediately, then do so. If it means the maid has to spend six hours cleaning rather than her usual two hours, then so be it. Have her do it. If your next renters show up, and they are still not done, instruct your maids to tell them to go out to lunch or dinner—on the owner. As for the costs (I think you guessed this one), take them out of the deposit of the messy renter, including the dinner you had to buy for the next renters. It's a cost associated with their damages. But, never consider this as an opportunity for you to make more money, only cover your costs. Here's another example.

> My maid showed up at my place, then called immediately and informed me that someone had smoked cigars in my unit. There is no excuse for that. Talk about ample warning! The no smoking policy is clearly stated on my websites, in my rental rules, on the sign on my front door, and on the nice framed note that says, "Our home is non-smoking, please respect it, feel free to use the ashtray located under the kitchen sink to smoke outside on the patio." But, apparently, they ignored all of that and smoked anyway. How was I going to get rid of the smell? It was nearly impossible to air out the place in the five hours between checkout and check-in. I followed all the steps above, had everything cleaned, and dinner for the next guests and all. Well, when I sent the letter with the deposit refund, these people called me. They unequivocally denied that they smoked in the unit; they admitted they smoked, but claimed they did so outside. They were arguing about having to pay the charges.

Now this becomes a he said/she said situation. Do I believe the renters or my maid? Maybe they *did* smoke outside but left the sliding door open and the smoke blew in. Or, maybe they smoked outside all week long, and then, as they were packing up, Dad had a stogie in his mouth as he was coming in and out. So what did I do? I stood behind my maid! I explained to the renter that I was sorry, but my loyalties have to be with my maid. I explained how she had worked for me for years and had never ever called me before. I explained that since I am not able to be there physically, my maid is the person responsible for making those judgment calls. The renter asked if she could then have my maid's phone number so she could discuss this with her. I said, "No. If you would like, I can have my maid sign a letter stating the damages." In the end, the renter was not pleased, but I stood firm. I still do not know the real story, but I have no reason not to believe my maid.

Cancellations

Cancellations are another issue that needs to be clearly defined in your rental rules. Keep in mind, you are not a big business, and your chances of re-renting a week grow exponentially lower as the date draws nearer. Some people choose to have a cancellation fee or re-rent fee. This fee would be $25–$50 dollars. Since you set the rules, you can make that figure anything you wish. If someone cancels, for no good reason (a good reason would be death in family, serious illness, call to military duty, etc.) then keep the deposit and/or any payments that you have received as per your rental rules. If you re-rent, then refund the moneys.

Lastly, there is also the option of putting that week up on one of the many auction websites, such as eBay. Just be sure to put in your auction notice that the winner must be approved by the property owner and comply with all rental rules and regulations. Otherwise you might end up getting the very kind of renters I've been advising you avoid! Read how one owner, Nadia, solved her cancellation problem:

> Nadia had rented her snowbird season (January to March) in April of the previous year for $1,000 per month + $200 damage deposit. In November, these guests stayed at her property for a long weekend. Upon returning, the renters called Nadia and explained that although her home was beautiful, and it was everything that she described, they decided to go to a totally different city for their three-month stay. Nadia's

rental rules required her snowbirds to pay in full 60 days prior to their rental date, and her cancellation for snowbird rentals was 180 days. She had every right to keep their full payment (but not the deposit since it was a damage deposit). Nadia explained to the renters that it would be very difficult to re-rent those dates since most snowbirds have secured their rentals by now. The renters clearly understood her dilemma as well as the rental policies. Fortunately for the renters, Nadia is very soft-hearted and felt really bad keeping their money. After all, she had spoken with the renters numerous times up to this point and felt as though they were friends. And ,they were so sweet. But on the flip side, Nadia could not afford to lose out on $3,000. The renters and Nadia came up with a great solution. Nadia agreed to do everything possible to try to re-rent those three months. One month passed and not a single renter called. When the renters and Nadia spoke next, the renters suggested that Nadia reduce the rental rate to $700 per month. They figured whatever portion of the rent they could recover would be better than nothing. Nadia changed her one-line ad on all her portal sites listings. She did not rent January, but did rent February and March and happily refunded the first snowbirds the $1,400 she received from the new renters.

Telephones & Long Distance Charges

The question of what to do about telephones and long-distance charges comes up often whenever I launch into a discussion about problems with renters. After all, you do not want to pay for your guests' toll charges. You can avoid long-distance charges by putting a long-distance blocker on your phone. This is available through your local phone company for a small fee. If you choose this option, be aware that it cannot be easily turned on and off. So if you are at your property, you will be forced to either use a calling card or your cell phone, even though you are in your own property.

Some owners are now considering unlimited or one-rate calling plans for their vacation properties. These are very reasonably priced and can be marketed as a selling tool: "free local and long-distance calls." But whatever you do, be sure to block out collect calls, person-to-person calls, and 900 numbers.

Complaints

It's hard to make generalizations about complaints, or give advice without knowing the specifics. However, I will tell you two of the most common complaints: the cleanliness of your place and the weather. Since we cannot control the weather, there's really nothing we can do about that one. "I am sorry it rained or didn't snow, I clearly understand, but if you choose to checkout early due to the weather, you must understand that you forfeit your rent." Clear as that!

Now about cleanliness. This is by far the most common complaint heard by owners. It is also the most frustrating. Our hands are tied as long-distance owners; we must completely rely on our cleaning staff.

The best way I can explain this is: have you ever told your child to go and clean his room? Of course you have. Then you ask, "Did you clean your room?" "Yes Mom!" Then you go up to check (because we know you cannot take *his* word), and you find the empty glasses from the last three nights on the bedside table, the bed still unmade, and dirty laundry draped across his chair! You look at your child and say, "I thought you said you cleaned your room?" And the child looks at you like you are absolutely insane. "Mom, I did clean my room! I vacuumed *and* dusted."

So is junior a liar? Not exactly. Your child did indeed clean … he just didn't pick up. That is *his perception* of clean. Although this is an exaggerated example, the point is, everyone's perception of *clean* is totally different. But you can't afford to leave any ambiguity about it when it comes to letting your cleaning service know exactly what it is that you expect.

To avoid cleanliness complaints after the fact, establish a check-in policy. In that policy, be sure to tell the renters, when you arrive, please check for cleanliness. If *anything* is not acceptable, then please call the maid immediately. If the renters do not notify you or the maid right away, then there is no way to rectify the problem. If they do not take the necessary steps, it is not your fault.

Since we put in all that time and effort, there is a lot of pride that we as owners have in our vacation homes. Sometimes, complaints can be taken as constructive criticism. Keep in mind, for every person that complains about something, there are probably five others who just let it go and said nothing. How many times have you eaten in a restaurant, and your food was not hot? There are some people who would send their plate back every time until it was perfect, and there are others who just wouldn't do anything. So, when you get a complaint, be sure to take it seriously, and if you can, resolve the problem as quickly as possible.

The People You Can Never Please

Unfortunately, there are people you can never please. Read about Matthew's guests who always complain:

> Christopher and his wife Erin come and stay every year at Matthew's ski lodge. They always stay for the first three weeks of the ski season. Every year, Matthew calls Christopher and Erin upon check-in, and every year, they complain and say, "Well, we had to do the usual cleaning before we moved our stuff in." All year, Matthew gets no complaints about the

cleanliness and has been using the same maid for five years; he knows she's good. Well, this year Matthew and his wife decided spend the week before the ski season at their rental place. The whole week, they cleaned everything possible. They pulled out the refrigerator, the stove, cleaned all the baseboards, had the carpets cleaned, the works! When he left, Matthew said to himself, "Ha! No way can Christopher and Erin complain this year." He does his usual phone call after they check-in and sure enough, he gets the same song and dance. The place was not clean!?!

Matthew and his wife shouldn't have wasted their time. Clearly, these renters were never going to be pleased (but I commend them for trying). The important part of the story is that in all those years none of the other guests complained. So if you get one or two renters who seem to be chronic whiners, and you're certain that their complaints are unfounded, just do your best to be a good listener, polite, and concerned. Just let it go in one ear and out the other.

Evictions

This is by far one of the scariest things that comes to mind when dealing with your vacation property. Evictions are even worse than dealing with damages because you are faced with a potential confrontation. This is the only reason that I can think of that would require you to jump on a plane or in your car to go and handle it yourself.

Thankfully, evictions are extremely rare, especially with by owner rentals, because we are screening our guests ourselves. The most common evictions is when there is miscommunication about the check-out time or date, for instance the guest thought they were staying until Sunday but their contract states Saturday and you have new renters due to check in on Saturday (this is another reason it's important to have signed contracts). Management companies sometimes have to evict due to disturbing the peace (partiers) but remember they don't really do much screening. I have never had to evict anyone nor has any owner I have ever taught, met, or spoken with. But again, it's best to be proactive on this topic. When you are faced with the dilemma of having to evict someone, chances are your blood pressure will be at full tilt. So do your research now, while you are clear-headed and make notes. Research the local policies on eviction for short-term renters. In most states, short-term and transient rentals fall under the same jurisdiction as your local hotels and motels. These laws tend to be quite different from the long-term lease laws, some of which are very restrictive, stating you cannot evict if the temperature outside is X degrees or lower, or during certain months of the year. Find out ahead of time if the police department will supply an officer for the eviction. If it comes to this, stand your ground.

Withholding Deposits

Now, if after you have done all due diligence to avoid problems, you still end up with an instance where you'll need to withhold the deposit, there are a couple of things you need to know.

First don't view damage deposits as a way to nickel and dime your renters out of some more cash. There are just some things that should be referred to as "the cost of doing business". Nor should it be used as a way to recoup money for your pain and aggravation. In other words, if a renter had made you angry, it does not give you the right to keep their deposit.

Second, if you keep a damage deposit or any portion of it, you should keep sound records of your exact costs associated with it. Let's say the renters left your place a filthy mess, you can only keep exactly the amount of money that your housekeeper charges for her extra time. If that time has gone over into the next renter's check in time and you have taken my suggestion to send the arriving inconvenienced guests a free meal, be sure to get a copy of that receipt for the meal for your records. In other words, be sure to keep good documentation!

The purpose of this chapter is not to scare you. As matter of fact, fear comes from ignorance. Now that you've read this chapter and have all of the facts you should realize that there is nothing at all to be afraid of. As I said, most of your guests will not be troublemakers. To the contrary, you are likely to become good friends with some of the people you rent to over the years. And if one of these days you do have a rotten experience with one of the bad apples (like that nasty kid you *still* remember from kindergarten), just deal with it and move on. Don't let it ruin your outlook on what otherwise is a very lucrative and rewarding business for you.

18

Networking with Other Owners

It really is true . . . there is strength in numbers. Networking with other owners is much more important than you may have thought. How many times have you borrowed a power tool or a cup of sugar from your neighbors at home? The same is true with your vacation home. And while you may not be swapping sugar, maybe you can bounce ideas off one another. Better yet, you can share lots of useful information, and help each other out. Remember, you share something in common with them, and you're basically in the same boat. Throughout this book, you will notice many references to other owners. In the sections about keys, maintenance, problem solving, pricing . . . come to think of it, I refer to other owners in just about every chapter, and that's not by coincidence. Networking is vital.

u find the other owners? In many cases, you will meet
n you are visiting your property. Don't worry if they
ompany, there are always things that these owners
many of the same things as you. If your property
…ion, you can obtain a list of owners directly from
…iation. Often the association will hold an annual homeowners meeting, a great opportunity to meet and socialize with your fellow
owners. I also try to find other owners who live in my hometown. This
is especially helpful for transporting small items and supplies.

If you are not in an association, you can find other owners from
the management companies or directly from their renters. Don't be
shy. If you see someone at his or her house, be neighborly, and strike
up a conversation. These guests may well know the owner. Or maybe
they *are* the owners.

Another great resource for meeting fellow owners is by attending
one of my seminars. **My seminars give you a golden opportunity to meet and
network with other vacation property owners.** I usually hold the seminars
in major metropolitan areas, although I do occasionally go to vacation
areas. Also be sure to check my website, www.howtorentbyowner.com,
I have a lot of useful information on there too, and I am adding new
information all the time.

And lastly, there are a couple of websites devoted to vacation
property owners and their networking needs. Three that come to
mind are Vacation Renters Owners Association (www.vroa.org),
VacationRentalOwner.com and http://groups.yahoo.com/group/vacation_
rentals/. These websites have a wealth of helpful information for vacation property owners as well as newsletters and discussion boards.
These websites have a wealth of helpful information for vacation
property owners as well as newsletters and discussion boards.

The best way to show you the value of networking is through a
real story. Read about how these two owners found each other and
how networking has helped them:

Denise lives in Anaheim, California. She owns a vacation home in Lake Tahoe and was eager to meet another owner. She went on the Internet and looked up Lake Tahoe. Then she searched for owners who live somewhere in the Anaheim area. That's where she met Sheryl. They conversed first via email, then over the telephone. Coincidentally, it turned out that Sheryl and Denise lived only a few blocks from one another at home too. They met five years ago and, believe it or not, have never been at their vacation homes in Tahoe at the same time. But every time Denise plans the trip, she calls Sheryl to see if she needs anything done, or transported. And, of course, Sheryl does the same for Denise.

These two truly work as a team of owners. They have done many things together and always work out discounts and deals. They take turns overseeing projects too. Sheryl always visits in the fall, so she orders the firewood and is there for delivery. Denise is always there in the spring, so she calls the chimney sweep and has both places done at the same time. One had all the screens replaced on her home, so the other did too. Their homes, even though very different, were built by the same builder. Denise's air conditioner went out one year, and she had to have it replaced. She told Sheryl. No, Sheryl didn't go and replace hers too, but since they had the same builder, and the houses were the same age, Sheryl now knew to be on the look out for this problem. It was very helpful information. They even have renters who call and want to book two places. What a perfect situation! And, naturally, they refer renters to one another too.

The important lesson from this story is that you don't have to do things for other owners with the express purpose of getting something back from them. Help them out simply because it's the right thing to do. And, chances are, you will find other owners who will do the same for you. What goes around truly does come around.

19

Final Notes from the Author

Think of this not as the end of the book, rather the start of a new adventure. This is where my advice ends and your actions begin.

Renting by owner isn't for everyone, but for most people it is the difference between being able to afford a vacation home and not. You now know how to share your dream home with others by managing it yourself, and having the rental income pay the mortgage, taxes, utilities, and maintenance. Oftentimes, owners get caught up in the management aspects of ownership. Don't let this encompass you. Schedule time for yourself to relax and enjoy your home.

I will close with my favorite article that continually inspires me. I read it as poetry, where I find many underlying hidden messages pertaining to all aspects of owning and managing my properties. Take the risk.

OF RISK AND REWARD

By Jack Simpson, real estate broker, columnist, and vacation homeowner.

"Life is richer and more rewarding for those who take risks to get what they want. Most all truly great achievements involve risk. This applies in the various fields of exploration, competitive sports, business, finance, even love and war. Real estate investing is no exception.

In the course of my business, I meet a lot of people who are looking for something more out of life. For many of them, it's a vacation rental home at the beach. The rewards are there to be had: pride of ownership, free personal use, rental income, and good potential for appreciation. But there are risks too. What if it doesn't rent? What if there's a hurricane? What of the unknown? Most bold, self-confident people go for it all—the risk and the reward. They buy. The timid talk themselves out of it. I feel sorry for them.

I am accustomed to taking risks, not only in real estate investing but in many other facets of life. If I see something I want, I go for it. Sometimes I hit. Sometimes I miss. But at least I am in there swinging. I have learned to savor the success and learn from the ones that don't work out. Along this line, I have some thoughts to share with you.

Control the risk. You can exert control over certain activities such as selecting your own investments or managing your own business. But you have absolutely no control over the spin of a roulette wheel or the draw of the lottery. I take risks but I don't gamble. There's a big difference.

Enjoy the risk. That's right—enjoy it. Risk is a challenge. It excites and sharpens the senses. Most people perform better under pressure. Some thrive on it. Who would play a golf course if it had no sand traps or water hazards? A world without challenge would be down right depressing.

Concentrate on your goal. Don't be distracted by obstacles and negative thoughts. Think about the golf course. You don't hit a hole in one if all you can think about is staying out of the rough. Whether you expect to win or to lose, you are probably right.

Accept all setbacks. Not every venture will be successful, but that doesn't mean it failed either. You fail only if you stop trying. Most every success story is full of setbacks along the way. They build character and make you a strong person.

Consider the alternative. Trying to eliminate the risks often creates other risks. Some people put all their money in a "safe" insured account only to see their buying power taken away by taxes and inflation. Ask yourself, 'What's the worst that can happen?' To me, the worst thing is seeing your life slip by without the risk and reward. That's sad.

We have all heard 'Nothing ventured, nothing gained,' 'Better to have loved and lost . . . ,' and those saddest of words '. . . it might have been.' But I believe Kris Kristofferson put it best when he wrote the song 'I'd rather be sorry for something I've done than for something I didn't do.' "

1

Forms

Throughout this book, there are many references to proper documentation and forms. It is very important, for both yourself and your renters, that you have these items. This is yet another way to make your business run smoothly. Consult an attorney to review your documents.

I recommend that you build a template for these forms in your word processing program. This can be easily accomplished by using popular programs such as Microsoft Word or WordPerfect. Save these templates, and use them over and over again. All forms, except the deposit refund, which is mailed with your deposit-refund check, can be emailed directly to your guest. I do not recommend that you email forms as attachments, however, because your recipient may not have a compatible program to open it. People worry about viruses too, and therefore, they often avoid downloading or opening attachments. Simply email these forms as plain text documents.

To convert your documents from word processing format to email, follow these simple steps:

1. Open your word processing document template.
2. Fill in the necessary information (i.e., today's date, names, dates of rental, etc.).
3. Select the whole document (Control+A) and choose copy (Control+C).
4. Next, open up a new email document, put your cursor in the body of the message, and choose paste (Control+V).

Pretty simple, isn't it?

Now, I am going to show you some samples of documents that you can use. Of course, you want to be sure to customize your forms to suit your property. Also, you may want to have an attorney look over your forms to be certain that you are properly covered.

Confirmation

The confirmation forms will be emailed to your renters upon booking. Do not send them as attachments. Remember to not accept a payment without the completed forms

```
Enclosed is our rental contract and rules. Please print,
read, sign, and send it along with your $200 deposit to
the address below. Thanks so much, and if you have any
questions, feel free to contact me.
    Thanks again,
    Christine

    Christine and Tom Karpinski
    Your Address
    Your city, State and Zip Code
```

Your Phone number

email Christine@HowtoRentByOwner.com

webpage www.howtorentbyowner.com

Today's Date,

Dear Mr. and Mrs. Guest,

Thank you for choosing our condominium for your vacation. We hope that you have a pleasant stay. The unit is located in the My Resort complex at 4567 Scenic Drive, Destin, Florida 3254, Unit #1234, Phone 850-654-3210.

Your confirmation is as follows:

Check-in date: June 19, 2004 after 3 P.M. CST (No early check-in please)

Check-out date: June 26, 2004 by 10 A.M. CST

Number of people in party: 2 adults, 2 children

After I receive your $200 deposit, your bill will be as follows:

Total bill $1,581.75 = $1,350 (rental rate) + $75 (cleaning fee) + $156.75 (11% Florida tax)

1st payment of $790.87 due April 19, 2004 (60 days prior)

2nd payment of $790.88 due June 5, 2004 (14 days prior)

As soon as I receive your final payment, I will send/call the lock box/key instructions.

Please sign and return 1 copy of this confirmation, and 1 copy of the rules.

Thanks! Have a great vacation!

Christine

Signature_____   Date_____

Rental Rules and Regulations

These will be emailed to your renters upon booking. Do not send them as attachments. Remember to not accept a payment without the completed forms. These forms are equally important as payment.

Use this form only as a model, you will want to add information regarding your property and it's hazards. Since I am not an attorney, it is very important have your attorney review your rental rules contract to ensure the terms and conditions of your contract comply with the state and local laws as well as rules and covenants where your property is located.

```
My Resort complex
4567 Scenic Drive, Destin, Florida 3254, Unit #1234,
Phone 850-654-3210.
```

1. CHECK-IN TIME IS AFTER 3 p.m. CST AND CHECK-OUT IS 10 a.m. CST. NO Early Check-ins. This agreement does not create a tenancy or residence. You must depart at the appropriate time.

2. This is a NON-SMOKING unit.

3. Pets are not permitted in rental units under any conditions.

4. We will not rent to vacationing students or singles under 25 years of age unless accompanied by an adult guardian or parent.

5. DAMAGE/RESERVATION DEPOSIT—A damage/reservation deposit of $200 is required. This must be received within seven (7) days of booking the reservation. The deposit automatically converts to a security/damage deposit upon arrival. The deposit is NOT applied toward rent; however, it is fully refundable within (14) days of departure, provided the following provisions are met.
   a. No damage is done to unit or its contents, beyond normal wear and tear.

b. No charges are incurred due to contraband, pets, or collection of rents or services rendered during the stay.

c. All debris, rubbish, and discards are placed in dumpster, and soiled dishes are placed in the dishwasher and cleaned. One load of laundry is started.

d. All keys are left on the kitchen table and unit is left locked.

e. All charges accrued during the stay are paid prior to departure.

f. No linens are lost or damaged.

g. NO early check-in or late checkout.

h. Parking passes are left inside the unit upon departure.

i. The renter is not evicted by the owner (or representative of the owner), the local law enforcement, or the security company employed by My Complex.

1. PAYMENT—An advance payment equal to 50% of the rental rate is required 60 days before arrival. The advance payment will be applied toward the rent. Please make payments in the form of traveler's checks, bank money orders, cashiers' checks, or personal checks payable to Your Name. The advance payment is not a damage deposit. The BALANCE OF RENT is due fourteen (14) days before your arrival date.

2. CANCELLATIONS—A sixty (60) day notice is required for cancellation. Cancellations that are made more than sixty (60) days prior to the arrival date will incur no penalty. Cancellations or changes that result in a shortened stay, that are made within 60 days of the arrival date, forfeit the full advance payment and damage/reservation

deposit. Cancellation or early departure does not warrant any refund of rent or deposit.

3. MONTHLY RESERVATION CANCELLATIONS— Monthly renters must cancel one hundred twenty (120) days prior to check-in. Monthly renters who make a change that results in a shortened stay must be made at least ninety (90) days prior to check-in.

4. MAXIMUM OCCUPANCY—The maximum number of guests per condominium is limited to eight (8) persons. An additional charge or $10.00 per person per night for guests in addition to eight (8) will be assessed.

5. THIS PROPERTY REQUIRES A THREE (3) NIGHT MINIMUM STAY. Longer minimum stays may be required during holiday periods. If a rental is taken for less than three days, the guest will be charged the three-night rate.

6. INCLUSIVE FEES—Rates include a one-time linen-towel set-up. Amenity fees are included in the rental rate.

7. NO DAILY MAID SERVICE—While linens and bath towels are included in the unit, daily maid service is not included in the rental rate; however it is available at an additional rate. We suggest you bring beach towels. We do not permit towels or linens to be taken from the units.

8. RATE CHANGES—Rates subject to change without notice.

9. FALSIFIED RESERVATIONS—Any reservation obtained under false pretense will be subject to forfeiture of advance payment, deposit, and/or rental money, and the party will not be permitted to check-in.

10. WRITTEN EXCEPTIONS—Any exceptions to the above mentioned policies must be approved in writing in advance.

11. PARKING PASSES—Parking passes are located inside the unit. Renters must display parking pass on the rear-view mirror at all times. Failure to display may result in towing of vehicle at renter's expense. Leave the parking passes inside the unit upon departure.

12. HURRICANE OR STORM POLICY—No refunds will be given unless:

    a. The National Weather Service orders mandatory evacuations in a "Tropical Storm/Hurricane Warning area" and/or

    b. A "mandatory evacuation order has been given for the Tropical Storm/Hurricane Warning" area of residence of a vacationing guest.

The day that the National Weather Service orders a mandatory evacuation order in a "Tropical Storm/Hurricane Warning," area, we will refund:

    a. Any unused portion of rent from a guest currently registered,

    b. Any unused portion of rent from a guest that is scheduled to arrive, and wants to shorten their stay, to come in after the Hurricane Warning is lifted; and

    c. Any advance rents collected or deposited for a reservation that is scheduled to arrive during the "Hurricane Warning" period.

By signing below, I agree to all terms and conditions of this agreement

Signature_____Date_____

For more Samples of rental rules, visit http://www.vroa.org/ (membership required) and http://www3.cyberrentals.com/lease1.html (free)

Pet Policy

For a sample pet policy addendum, visit the Humane Society's website at www.hsus.org/ace/11803 or www.rentwithpets.org.

Directions & Arrival Policy

Send directions, arrival policy, departure information, and emergency information as one document.

```
    I received your final payment. Thanks! Enclosed are
all the directions you will need to get to and into the
condo.
    Have a great time,
    Christine
```

Directions To My Resort complex Give clear directions from all points, north, south, east, west, airport, etc. Be sure to include landmarks before and after your property (in case they passed it).

My Resort Complex is located at 4567 Scenic Drive, Destin, Florida 3254, Unit #1234. The resort is located east of Destin (proper). It is between the Wal-Mart and the Silver Sands Outlet Mall.

There is an entrance into My Resort Complex from the main road through Destin, Hwy 98, or you can access the resort from Scenic Drive. The security gate code is 123456.

Coming from the Airport, take a left out of the airport, go to the end of the road, and turn left onto State Rt 31. Once you pass the Burger King, take a right on to the Mid-Bay Bridge (toll road $2). At the end of the bridge, take a left, and follow directions coming from west.

Coming from the west, you'll pass Wal-Mart (on left) and Home Depot (on left). After signs for Miramar Beach watch for the My Resort Complex sign on the right. If you get to the Silver Sands Outlet Mall, you've gone too far. Once in the complex, take your first right, then proceed to the condo buildings.

Coming from the east, pass Sandestin, then turn left, at the first sign for the beaches, onto Scenic Drive (Silver Sands Outlet mall on right). Stay on Scenic Drive, aprox. 2 miles. My Resort Complex will be on the right (just passed Neighbor).

Once in the Resort, proceed to Condo Bldg #1. We're unit #1234 (second floor).

The lock box code is 01234, take the keys out, and keep them with you at all times. When you leave, **PLEASE leave the keys on the kitchen table.** No early check-in is allowed.

The beach gate code is 9876.

When you arrive, please inspect the condo for cleanliness, if ANYTHING is not acceptable; do not hesitate to call the maid, Mrs. Clean at 850-987-6543 (home) or 876-5432 (cell).

Thanks and have a great vacation!

Departure Information

Before departure please be sure to do the following:
- Take out all trash to the dumpster.
- Start one load of laundry (sheets or towels).
- Load and run the dishwasher.
- Sign our guest book.
- Leave the keys on the kitchen table (Lock the door w/the doorknob lock)
- Leave by 10 A.M.
- Have a safe journey home.

Emergency Information

Be sure to have all the following information on both your directions and posted somewhere on your property. I copied mine on pretty paper, framed it, and put it near my telephone in my unit.

In case of emergency, dial **911**.
Poison Control 654-3210
You are in Walton County.
My Resort, in Destin, Florida
The address is . . .
4567 Scenic Drive,
Destin, Florida 32541
Unit #1234
Phone 850-654-3210

If you have trouble with the unit,
call the owners—Tom and Christine Karpinski.
Call collect, 770-592-7860.

We can also be reached on our cell phones . . .
770-123-4567(Christine) or 770-234-5678 (Tom)

If you cannot get a hold of us, please call the maid,
Mrs. Clean at 850-987-6543 (home) or 876-5432 (cell).

Vacation Tips

You will want to include some useful vacation area tips. Notice I have covered, shopping, restaurants, and attractions as well as some area dangers.

You can find many local area tips in a book on my coffee table. Here are a few personal favorites for the area:

When you go to the outlet mall, make your first stop the mall office, open until 6:30 P.M. (located behind the mall, accessible from Morgan's). They have a book-let called the "passport book," which is full of all sorts of coupons for most of the stores . . . also if the men decide to go shopping too and get tired, they have billiard room in the upstairs of the food court. If you take the kids along, Morgan's also has a game room. In the passport book, there's usually a coupon for buy $5 worth of tokens—get $5 free!

Deepsea fishing is great in Destin. If the guys like deep sea fishing . . . this is a "must" for them.

Seaside is a nice little village east down 98 . . . watch for the signs, you'll take a right. Seaside is a very upscale area that's fun to go to "dream" about when you win the lottery. They have a bunch of artsy shops . . . but things are very expensive . . . just a fun place to look around.

Keep your eyes open if on the beach at dusk or dawn, we very often see dolphins swimming right off shore. If the dolphins come in close, which they do occasion-ally, do not get in the water and try to touch them. Please respect that they are wildlife. It is illegal to touch the dolphins (we humans have germs that harm the dolphins).

A fun "cheap" thing to do is to rent the ocean kayaks off the beach. Morning is usually the best time; the waters are generally calmer. The kayaks are very easy to maneuver, and it's only around $10/hour.

There are a lot of great restaurants in the area. The Back Porch is one of our favorites. It's located in Destin. Depending on the season, it can be very crowded, so be prepared to wait. They do have a playground on the beach for the kids to play in while waiting. I recommend you bring a change of clothes for the little ones; it's tough to resist the temptation to play near the water, and it's better to be prepared than to get upset when they inevitably get wet. Remember you're on vacation, there's no use stressing about it!

If you want to cook up a seafood feast, my favorite store is called Shrimper's. To get there, go east on 98, past the outlet mall about 6 or 8 miles, and it's on the left-hand side, past Bayou Bill's . . . They have the freshest fish and shrimp and great prices . . . A local "specialty" is the smoked tuna dip; it's great on crackers as an appetizer. Also, if you can get your hands on "red shrimp," they're a must try! Boil them in water for 1½ MINUTES (no more, no less!), and then dip them in drawn butter, and you'll think you're eating lobster . . . Typically "reds" are only available on Tuesdays. Shrimper's also has the "best" key lime pie around!

There is also another seafood market that has now hired a full-time chef to prepare things that you can cook at home. It is supposed to make it easy to make "home cooked gourmet food." It's called Destin Ice, and it's located on Hwy 98 to the west on the right, almost all the way down to the bridge to the island.

I recently discovered there is a new Dollar store on HWY 98 that has a lot of useful items all for $1. It's a great place to pick up odds and ends along with sand toys. It's located west of the condo, just past the Home Depot on the right, in the shopping center with Office Max/Depot.

Recently there have been some ocean-related deaths along the gulf coast. Please pay attention to the flags

on the beach. If there is a RED FLAG, do NOT swim. The
rip tides (rip currents) have been very strong. If you
by chance do get caught in a rip tide, swim parallel to
the beach. Our beach does NOT have lifeguards.

Deposit Refund Letter

Send the deposit refund letter with the refund check after you have
confirmation from your maid that there was no damage or theft. A
nice personal touch would be to hand write this in a thank you card
and send a business card magnet so your renters can contact you
again.

```
    Your name
    Your address
    Your City, State, Zip
    Your Phone Number
    Your email address
    Your webpage address http://your website address.
com
    Today's date


    Dear Mr. and Mrs. Renter,
    Thank you for choosing our condominium for your
vacation. We hope that you had a pleasant stay. The
condo was left in good condition;, therefore, enclosed
you'll find your $200 deposit refund.
    If you wish to rent again, just call/email me. I
will start taking spring 2003 reservations in Septem-
ber 2002. I do book up quickly so just keep that in
mind if you're set on particular dates.
    Looking forward to hearing from you again.
    Thanks again!
    Christine
```

Cleaning Checklist

When dealing with your maids and cleaning staff, it's best to have a clear, concise list of duties. It's best to be a specific as possible. Post these somewhere in your property; the inside of a closet door works well.

Kitchen

❑ Clean appliances, counters, cabinets, table, and chairs.

❑ Clean, scrub, and sanitize sinks, countertops, and backsplashes.

❑ Clean range top and wipe out inside of oven.

❑ Clean appliance exteriors, including the inside of toaster and coffee maker.

❑ Clean inside and outside of refrigerator and microwave oven.

❑ Wash floor.

❑ Empty dishwasher, and quickly organize cupboards.

❑ Restock auto dish detergent, liquid dish soap, coffee filters, and trash bags.

❑ Put out 2 clean dishtowels, and a new dish rag/sponge.

Living Room

❑ Clean, dust, and vacuum.

❑ Dust window sills and ledges.

❑ Dust furniture, blinds, picture frames, knickknacks, ceiling fans, and lamps.

❑ Vacuum carpets or wash floor.

❑ Vacuum furniture, including under seat cushions.

❑ Check sofa bed for dirty linens.

❑ Wash windows on sliding glass doors.

❑ Empty and clean wastebaskets.

❑ Be sure to leave clean linens for the sofa bed.

Bathrooms

❑ Clean, scrub and sanitize showers, bathtubs, vanity, sinks, and backsplashes.

❑ Clean mirrors.

❑ Clean and sanitize toilets.

❑ Polish chrome.

❑ Wash floors and tile walls.

❑ Empty wastebasket.

❑ Replenish liquid hand soap.

❑ Supply clean linens, # hand towels, # washcloths, # bath towels, and 1 shower mat.

Other areas

❑ Be sure washer and dryer are empty; clean out lint trap.

❑ Check light bulbs, change if necessary.

❑ Once per month, change furnace filter.

❑ Wipe off patio set, clean barbeque grill.

❑ Notify owner immediately if you notice any damages, missing items, or if the place was left excessively dirty.

2

Websites

Listing sites (portal sites) dedicated to listing vacation properties.
Listed alphabetically.

www.10kvacationrentals.com
www.1-2-c.com
www.1stvacations.com
www.4beachnuts.com
www.5starvacationrentals.com
www.a1vacations.com
www.allrentalsbyowner.com
www.alluradirect.com
www.aroundfrance.com
www.availablevacations.com
www.beachhouse.com
www.cafegetaway.com
www.central-oregon.com/vac_rent
www.choice1.com
www.condorenthelp.com
www.costaholidays.com
www.cottagenet.co.uk
www.cottageportal.com

www.cvoa.com
www.cyberrentals.com
www.erhomes.com
www.findvacationrentals.com
www.floridavacations.com
www.francevoila.com
www.goin2travel.com
www.goto-france.com
www.greatfamilyrentals.com
www.greatrentals.com
www.greatvacationhomes.com
www.gulfcoastrentals.com
www.gulivers.com
www.holidaylets.net
www.holidaypropertyguide.com
www.holswap.com
www.idealvacationrentals.com
www.ifb.com

www.indvr.com
www.islandtime.com/rentals
www.ivponline.com
www.jcn1.com/mbamford/pets_allowed
www.krazymoose.com
www.letsroc.com
www.lodging4vacations.com
www.mexicovacations.com
www.mountain-lodging.com
www.mycaliforniavacations.com
www.mycoloradovacations.com
www.myfloridavacations.com
www.myhawaiivacations.com
www.mynorthcarolinavacations.com
www.mysouthcarolinavacations.com
www.nyvacationrentals.com
www.onlinevacationrentals.com
www.ownerdirect.com
www.perfectplaces.com
www.petfriendly.ca
www.petfriendlytravel.com
www.petswelcome.com
www.ppbo.com
www.realadventures.com
www.rent101.com
www.rent1online.com
www.rentalo.com

www.rentalsfrance.com
www.rentalsinthepoconos.com
www.rentmyhome.com
www.runawayrentals.com
www.sciway.net/tourism/vrentals.html
www.shorevacations.com
www.slowtrav.com
www.summerinitaly.com
www.tahoesbest.com
www.timeawayrentals.com
www.travelpets.com/content/listing.htm
www.ultimatevacationrentals.com
www.vacanca.com
www.vacationpalmsprings.com
www.vacationparadise.com
www.vacationrentals.com
www.vacationrentals411.com
www.vacationrentalspaces.com
www.vacationvalley.com
www.vacationworldwide.net
www.villas2000.com
www.villa-vacation.com
www.vlbo.com
www.vrbo.com
www.vrworldwide.com
www.weneedavacation.com
www.worldwidevillas.com

APPENDIX

3

Special Discounts

The following companies have offered discounts to anyone who purchases this book.

Portal Sites

www.10kvacationrentals.com	14-month subscription for the price of 12 months. Use code HTRBO-020404.
www.1stvacations.com	Discount coupon for any renter or owner (one per family) http://rentalsfrance.com/coupon.
www.4beachnuts.com	$24 off advertised rates.
www.a1vacations.com	5% discount on first webpage for new customers only, if you specify the Referral Code CK-123104.
www.cafegetaway.com	50% discount off first year. New listings only.
www.choice1.com	30% Silver Package rates ($70 savings!). Enter offer code SIBRBOOK. New listings only, cannot be combined with any other offer.
www.costaholidays.com	20% special discount for the first 2 years, new listings only.

www.cottageportal.com	3 FREE additional months added to any new paid listing. Enter HTRBO in "referral code" when joining.
www.cyberrentals.com	3 free months added to your new listing and free mouse pad! Mention "How to Rent by Owner Book" on the online form.
www.findvacationrentals.com	$25 Off New Listings Only. Enter 25OFF in the Promo Code field.
www.francevoila.com	Discount coupon for any renter or owner (one per family) http://rentalsfrance.com/coupon.
www.greatfamilyrentals.com	$40 new listing only. Use 2004Howto in the promotion box.
www.greatrentals.com	1 month free advertising, code kar004.
www.gulfcoastrentals.com	$10 off first year new listings only Must write '"I decided to list with Gulf Coast after reading How to Rent by Owner book" in promotion box.
www.idealvacationrentals.com	$20 off one year standard or deluxe listing email: webmaster@idealvacationrentals.com, and "I read about your site in How To Rent By Owner."
www.krazymoose.com	25% off– Mention "How to Rent by Owner book offer."
www.mountain-lodging.com	50% off annual fee if you are the first listing in your state. $30 off first year listing. Mention "How to Rent by Owner book."
www.mycaliforniavacations.com	$25 Off New Listings Only. Enter 25OFF in the Promo Code field.
www.mycoloradovacations.com	$25 Off New Listings Only. Enter 25OFF in the Promo Code field.
www.myfloridavacations.com	$25 Off New Listings Only. Enter 25OFF in the Promo Code field.
www.myhawaiivacations.com	$25 Off New Listings Only. Enter 25OFF in the Promo Code field.
www.mynorthcarolinavacations.com	$25 Off New Listings Only. Enter 25OFF in the Promo Code field.
www.mysouthcarolinavacations.com	$25 Off New Listings Only. Enter 25OFF in the Promo Code field.
www.nyvacationrentals.com	$20 off when upgrading to a featured listing. Mention XRBO.

www.onlinevacationrentals.com	$40 in free clicks. Write "HTRBO" in the offer box. The initial deposit is waved.
www.perfectplaces.com	25% off new listings. Mention discount code "Karpinski"
www.petfriendlytravel.com	10% discount new listing. Mention this book when registering your property.
www.ppbo.com	25% off first year's listing Enter coupon code 25 HTRBO
www.rent101.com	20% off your first year when you mention discount code rbo.
www.rentalo.com	1 Free Month when subscribing to any of our Premium Subscriptions. Mention promotional code: CK upon subscribing.
www.rentalsfrance.com	Discount coupon for any renter or owner (one per family) http://rentalsfrance.com/coupon.
www.rentalsinthepoconos.com	$20 off when upgrading to a featured listing. Mention XRBO.
www.shorevacations.com	$20 off when upgrading to a featured listing. Mention XRBO.
www.summerinitaly.com	Front-page position for one year to all readers who mention "How to Rent by Owner book."
www.tahoesbest.com	One FREE month on New Standard Annual Listing, reference code "How to Rent by Owner."
www.timeawayrentals.com	50% off first year's listing. Use coupon code PROCK50
www.vacationrentals.com	60-day free trail plus 30-day grace period to submit payments.
www.vacationrentalspaces.com	3 Additional Months Free, 1st year new listings, Write "KAR-01."
www.vacationworldwide.net	Buy 1 year get 1 free on any annual membership level. Mention this book.
www.vrbo.com	1 free extra month of service, new listings only. Enter code ""HTRBO"" in the "referred by" field when joining.

Other Companies

www.atlantatradinggroup.com	Atlanta Trading Group offers speciality and custom funishings, stone and statuary. World-wide delivery available. Mention this book and receive 10% off total order.
www.hotspotmanagement.com	Sales tax filing service. 20% off first year, call in with code CK04.
www.journalsunlimited.com	20% any guest books
www.nokey.com	Mention "How to Rent by Owner book" to receive 10% off your order.
www.rent1online.com	One free week of live operator reservation service. Great for times when you are unavailable. Mention "How to Rent By Owner".
www.tksvacationrental.com	Builds, manages and promotes personal web sites for vacation rental owners. Mention this book for 1 free half hour consultation.
www.trustetc.com	A leader in Self-Directed IRAs. $25 off Set-Up Fee.
www.thevacationexchange.com	Free photo included with membership. ($20 value) Reference Code: SB10 (Please put reference code after Surname on the application).
www.vroa.org	$10 discount on first year use promotion code "64461."

4

Vacation Exchange Websites

Trade your vacation property with other owners around the world.
Listed alphabetically.

Aha!Go

www.ahago.com
Home exchange and vacation rentals. Initial use free, small charge after you actually make an exchange. Planning tools include a true distance finder.

Blue-Home

www.blue-home.com
Listings for home and apartment exchange worldwide. Free search. In English, French, and Spanish.

B-O-S-S Home Exchange

www.b-o-s-s.com
Panama City, FL-based home exchange company offering home exchange services throughout the world.

Christian Home Exchange

www.christianhomexchange.com
U.S.-based Christian home exchange network.

Digsville

www.digsville.com
U.S-based home and hospitality exchange featuring properties on six continents. Site features a search, rating system, lively community, customer service, and free membership.

Erhomes	www.erhomes.com Site includes rentals as well. Listing a home exchange wish is free.
ExchangeHomes	www.exchangehomes.com Exchange homes, swap lifestyles, and trade cultures. Home exchange provides an opportunity to experience foreign lifestyles in a way tourists never do—for free.
ExchangePlaces.com	www.exchangeplaces.com Offers information on vacation rentals and home exchanges worldwide.
HomeExchange.Com	www.homeexchange.com Offers international home exchange search without being a member.
Home Invite	www.homeinvite.com Global home exchange site that requires registration but free to use.
HomeLink	www.swapnow.com Color directories and interactive database of home exchange listings.
Intalet Holiday Home Exchange	www.intalet.co.uk International home exchange. Requires registration.
Interline Homeswaps	www.interlinehomeswaps.net Free site that lists your home for swapping with others in the travel industry.
Invented City Home Exchange	www.invented-city.com Home exchange listings, with photographs, in 40+ countries around the world.
Leisure Property Exchange LLC	www.leisurepropertyexchange.com Coordinates vacation home exchanges.
People Travel the World	www.peopletraveltheworld.com Offers yacht and boat exchange on a home exchange basis. Includes planning guide.
Seniors Home Exchange	www.seniorshomeexchange.com Home exchanges exclusively for over age 50 group.
Singles Home Exchange International	www.singleshomeexchange.com Worldwide home exchanges and apartment exchanges for singles, single parent, couples, and small families.

Sun Swap	www.sunswap.com Database of homes for trading, house swapping, and vacation home exchanges.
The Traveler Exchange	www.traveler-exchange.com Free online hospitality exchange. Registration required.
Trading-Homes	www.trading-homes.com Members have online access to listings of other members from all over the world who want to exchange their homes for their next vacation.
Trippolis	www.trippolis.com Home exchange site for regions around the world. Forum, chat and FAQ.
The Vacation Exchange Network	www.thevacationexchange.com Members exchange their vacation homes and condos.
Vacation Homes Unlimited	www.swapngo.co.uk Established in 1986. Both Internet and printed directory memberships available.
Vacation Point Exchange	www.vacationpointexchange.com Exchange a stay at your vacation home or condo for a stay at someone 'else's—worldwide.

5

State Sales Tax Offices

Contact for information on collecting and paying sales tax.

Alabama	www.ador.state.al.us/salestax/index.html
Alaska	www.dced.state.ak.us/dca/LOGON/tax/tax-sales.htm
Arizona	www.revenue.state.az.us
Arkansas	www.state.ar.us/dfa/odd/salestax_index.html
California	www.boe.ca.gov/sutax/faqscont.htm
Colorado	www.revenue.state.co.us/TPS_Dir/wrap.asp?incl=salestaxforms
Connecticut	www.ct.gov
Delaware	www.state.de.us/revenue/index.htm
Florida	www.myflorida.com/dor/taxes/sales_tax.html
Georgia	www2.state.ga.us/departments/dor/salestax/index.shtml
Hawaii	www.state.hi.us/tax
Idaho	www2.state.id.us/tax/questions.htm (see Sales & Use Tax)
Illinois	www.revenue.state.il.us
Indiana	www.ai.org/dor/taxforms/s-wforms.html
Iowa	www.state.ia.us/tax/taxlaw/taxtypes.html#sales
Kansas	www.ksrevenue.org
Kentucky	revenue.ky.gov/salestax_info.htm
Louisiana	www.rev.state.la.us/sections/business/sales.asp#sales
Maine	www.state.me.us/revenue/salesuse/homepage.html

Maryland	business.marylandtaxes.com/taxinfo/salesanduse/default.asp
Massachusetts	www.dor.state.ma.us/help/guides/stg_form.htm
Michigan	www.michigan.gov/treasury
Minnesota	www.taxes.state.mn.us/taxes/sales/index.shtml
Mississippi	www.mstc.state.ms.us/taxareas/sales/main.htm
Missouri	www.dor.mo.gov/tax/business/sales
Montana	discoveringmontana.com/revenue/css/3forbusinesses/ 01taxeslicensesfees/g-salestax/default.asp
Nebraska	www.revenue.state.ne.us/salestax.htm
Nevada	tax.state.nv.us
New Hampshire	www.state.nh.us/revenue/meals+rentals/index.htm
New Jersey	www.state.nj.us/treasury/taxation/index.html?hotelfee. htm~mainFrame
New Mexico	www.state.nm.us/tax
New York	www.tax.state.ny.us/Forms/sales_cur_forms.htm
North Carolina	www.dor.state.nc.us/taxes/sales
North Dakota	www.state.nd.us/taxdpt/salesanduse
Ohio	tax.ohio.gov/business_taxes_sales.html
Oklahoma	www.oktax.state.ok.us/btforms.html
Oregon	www.dor.state.or.us
Pennsylvania	www.revenue.state.pa.us/revenue/taxonomy/taxonomy. asp?DLN=3637
Rhode Island	www.tax.state.ri.us/info/synopsis/syntoc.htm
South Carolina	www2.sctax.org/esales
South Dakota	www.state.sd.us/drr2/Revenue.html
Tennessee	www.state.tn.us/revenue/tntaxes/salesanduse.htm
Texas	www.window.state.tx.us/taxinfo/sales/new_business.html
Utah	tax.utah.gov/sales/index.html
Vermont	www.state.vt.us/tax/index.htm
Virginia	www.tax.state.va.us/site.cfm?alias=SalesUseTax
Washington	dor.wa.gov/content/citizen/citizn_saleuse.asp
Washington D.C.	dc.gov/index.asp
West Virginia	www.state.wv.us/taxdiv
Wisconsin	www.dor.state.wi.us/html/taxsales.html
Wyoming	revenue.state.wy.us/doclistout.asp?div=12&dtype=6

6

Learning Centers

Here is a list of learning centers across the U.S. where you can take many short courses on computer skills and website design. Often you will find Christine Karpinski's "How to Purchase Vacation Properties" and "How to Rent by Owner" seminars in these locations.

Albany, NY: The Knowledge Network, www.knowledgenetwork.org

Albuquerque, NM: Sageways, www.sageways.org

Atlanta, GA: The Knowledge Shop, www.knowledgeshopatlanta.com/

Boston, MA: Boston Learning Society, www.bostonlearningsociety.com

Calgary, Alberta: The Learning Annex, www.learningannex.com

Chicago, IL: Discovery Center, www.discoverycenter.com

Denver, CO: Colorado Free University, www.freeu.com

Edmonton, Alberta: The Learning Annex, www.learningannex.com

Houston, TX: Leisure Learning Unlimited, www.llu.com

Los Angeles, CA: The Learning Annex, www.learningannex.com

Minneapolis MN: The Learning Annex, www.learningannex.com

Monterey CA: Center-for, www.center-for.com

New York, NY: The Learning Annex, www.learningannex.com

Newport, RI: Newport Learning Connection, www.newportlearningconnection.com

Orlando, FL: The Knowledge Shop, www.knowledgeshoporlando.com

Philadelphia, PA: Mt. Airy Learning Tree, www.mtairylearningtree.org

Providence, RI: Learning Connection—Providence, www.learnconnect.com

Rochester, NY: Rochester Info-Courses, www.infocourses.com

Sacramento, CA: Learning Exchange, www.learningexchange.com

San Diego, CA: The Learning Annex, www.learningannex.com

San Francisco, CA: The Learning Annex, www.learningannex.com

Seattle, WA: Discover U, www.discoveru.org

Tampa FL: Baywinds, www.baywinds.net

Toronto, Ontario: The Learning Annex, www.learningannex.com

Vancouver, BC: The Learning Annex, www.learningannex.com

Washington, DC: First Class, www.takeaclass.org

APPENDIX

7

Recommendations

Please note there are people and companies that have given me permission to use their copyrighted information. I only contacted companies that I truly believe in. Below is a list of their businesses and contact information.

Holiday Isle Properties
Jack Simpson
842 Highway 98 East
Destin, FL 32541
850-837-0092
www.holidayisle.net

Holiday Isle Properties offers real estate sales, full-service vacation property management and partnership programs at 0% commission.

Equity Trust Company

225 Burns Road

Elyria, OH 44035

440-323-5491

http://trustetc.com

The Equity Trust Company is a leading provider of truly self-directed Individual Retirement Accounts (IRAs) and small business retirement plans. Clients at Equity Trust have the option to invest their retirement funds in areas where they have knowledge and expertise. Equity Trust IRA investment options include real estate IRAs, mortgages/deeds of trust, and private placement IRAs.

Amy Ashcroft Greener

Copywriting, Photography, & Image Development

17366 Ida West Rd.

Petersburg, MI 49270

734-279-1140

thecreativeedge4copy@yahoo.com

www.swayingpines.com

Writing and image consulting services for vacation rental property owners.

Jeff Cutler

5909 Peachtree Dunwoody Road, Ste 710

Atlanta, GA 30328

877-587-5363

http://yourbestrate.net

Your Best Rate Financial is a direct mortgage lender and offers home loan mortgage financing in many states.

Supra, Division of GE Interlogix

4001 Fairview Industrial Drive SE

Salem, OR 97302

503-589-8660

www.ge-keysafe.com

Manufacturers of KeySafe - C3 Portable lock boxes.

Broderick Perkins

San Jose, CA

info@deadlinenews.com

www.deadlinenews.com

Broderick Perkins, is executive editor of San Jose, CA-based DeadlineNews. Com, an editorial content and consulting firm. Perkins has been a consumer and real estate journalist for 25 years.

Bart Meltzer

269 Mt. Herman Rd.

Scotts Valley, CA 95066

bart@kali-kona.com

www.Rent1on.line.com

www.trykona.com

Rent1online.com offers organization and reservation software solutions for vacation property owners.

Index

About the Author

Christine Hrib Karpinski's first and most important job is as a stay-at-home mom. She fell into teaching about vacation properties only by chance. Realizing that there was no way to she could afford to buy a vacation home using a management company, she started "renting by owner." Not only was she successful, others wanted to know how to do it too. She started writing a column in *Gulf Coast Condo Owner Magazine*. From there, the rest as they say, is history.

When she's not teaching or taking care of her family, you'll find her in a pottery studio creating with her hands, singing in her church choir, or relaxing on the beach in Destin, Florida.

Christine was born in Syracuse, New York. Currently she resides in Woodstock, Georgia with her husband Tom, son Zachary, and two Nova Scotia Duck Tollers, Trumpet and Piccolo.

Order Form

ONLINE ORDERS:	www.HowToRentByOwner.com
FAX ORDERS:	770-592-0193
TELEPHONE ORDERS:	Call 770-592-7860 (have your credit card ready.)
E-MAIL ORDERS:	orders@HowToRentByOwner.com
POSTAL ORDERS:	Kinney Pollack Press
	PMB 278 2295 Towne Lake Parkway, Suite 116
	Woodstock, GA 30189, USA
	Telephone 770-592-7860

TITLE	PRODUCT	PRICE	QUANTITY	SUBTOTAL
How to Rent Vacation Properties By Owner	Book	$26	_____	_____
The Vacation Rental Organizer	Book	$19	_____	_____
The Essentials of Owning and Renting Vacation Properties	DVD	$39	_____	_____
The DVD Seminar + The Rental Organizer—Save $9!		$49	_____	_____
The Book + The DVD Seminar—Save $6!		$59	_____	_____
YOUR BEST BUY!—The Book + The DVD Seminar + The Rental Organizer—Save $15		$69	_____	_____
		Sales Tax*		_____
		Shipping**		_____
		TOTAL		_____

Sales Tax: Please add 6% tax for products shipped to Georgia addresses.
***US: Add $5 for first product and $3 for each additional product.**
International: $ 10 for first product and $6 for each additional product.

Shipping

Name: _____

Address: _____

City, State Zip: _____

Telephone: _____

E-mail address: _____

Payment

❏ Check enclosed   ❏ VISA   ❏ MasterCard

Card Number _____

Exp. Date _____

Signature _____

Name on card _____

Billing Address _____

_____